HOW TO BE THE FAMILY CFO

4 Simple Steps to Put Your Financial House in Order

Kim Snider

GREENLEAF
BOOK GROUP PRESS

Published by Greenleaf Book Group Press
Austin, Texas
www.gbgpress.com

Distributed by Greenleaf Book Group LLC

For ordering information or special discounts for bulk purchases, please contact Greenleaf Book Group LLC at PO Box 91869, Austin, TX 78709 (512) 891-6100.

Design and composition by Greenleaf Book Group LLC
Cover design by Greenleaf Book Group LLC

Publisher's Cataloging-In-Publication Data
(Prepared by The Donohue Group, Inc.)

Snider, Kim.
   How to be the family CFO : four simple steps to put your financial house in order / Kim Snider. -- 1st ed.

   p. ; cm.

   Includes bibliographical references.
   ISBN: 978-1-929774-74-6 .

1. Finance, Personal--United States. 2. Financial security--United States. 3. Budgets, Personal--United States. 4. Investments--United States. I. Title.

HG179 .S65 2009
332.024/01   2008931125

Printed in the United States of America on acid-free paper

11 12 13 14 15 16   10 9 8 7 6 5 4 3

First Edition

This book is dedicated to Mother and Mel, Pam A., and my husband Jim. Without you, there would have been no happy ending to this story.

CONTENTS

INTRODUCTION

Failure is just the opportunity to begin again more intelligently.

—Henry Ford

TODAY I AM AN author and radio talk show host. I speak publicly on the subject of saving and investing for retirement. I have taught my cash flow investment method to thousands of investors. But all of that came later. Originally, I just had to solve this problem for myself: "How do I make sure I never find myself in this position again?"

The "position" I am referring to is having gone from being rich to being flat broke in less than two years! Maybe some of you can relate.

Twenty years ago, I went to work for a small computer supplies wholesaler. At the time, they were doing about $36 million a year in sales. I was just a few years out of college and started as a clerk in the purchasing department.

Over time, I rose up through the ranks, ultimately reaching the level of senior management. With each promotion came additional responsibilities and pay. Some of that pay came in the form of stock options.

In January 1995 the company went public. By then, they were closing in on $500 million a year in sales and would soon reach a billion.

At the moment my employer's ticker symbol crossed the tape for the very first time, I suddenly had more money than most people dream of having even after a lifetime of work. I was 31 years old.

I knew nothing about investing or taking care of money. In fact, at the time the company went public, I was basically living paycheck to paycheck (albeit a fairly large one) just like everyone else.

I had gone to some of the finest schools our country has to offer. I had business law in high school, and I graduated from college with a degree in business. I took several classes in corporate finance. I could do double entry accounting, tell you about supply and demand curves, program a computer, and read a novel in French. But nowhere along the way did anyone ever sit me down and explain the basics of personal finance or investing. Strange, isn't it?

So, having grown up on television commercials, I did the thing that seemed most reasonable. I went to one of those big brokerage firms and asked them what I should do with the money. They told me they had brokers who would be more than happy to manage that money on my behalf.

Cool! Problem solved. Abdicate responsi—I mean, hire someone else to handle it.

Mind you, I didn't just pull a name out of a phone book. I got a recommendation from the lead underwriter on our public offering. My broker came highly recommended and worked for the parent company of the investment bank that took our company public. Without naming names, I'll just say that unless you have lived your whole life under a rock, you know the name of this firm.

In all fairness, I will be the first to admit that I didn't handle my side very well. I spent a lot of money on really dumb things. In fact, I quit my job and proceeded to have a really good time. That is what you do when you are young and foolish and feeling bulletproof. But you know what? The broker did his fair share of dumb things too.

I didn't understand what he was doing. Frankly, I didn't even try to understand what he was doing. After all, he was supposed to be the expert. Whatever he suggested, I agreed to. How could I not? I didn't have any facts to base a decision on one way or the other. I was like a leaf floating along in the river, going wherever the current might take me. And where it took me was over the falls!

Less than two years later, I was dead broke. I had to admit to God and the world that I had screwed up the opportunity of a lifetime. That is a pretty bitter pill to swallow when you look at yourself in the mirror each morning.

I didn't have a penny to my name, I was in debt up to my eyeballs, and all my cool toys were repossessed. I sold my swanky high-rise condo at a terrible loss just to stay out of foreclosure. My credit was wrecked and I had no job. I couldn't even afford to buy dog food for my dog.

The worst part about it was having to go to my own mother and ask for a loan so I could eat. No, that wasn't quite the worst. The worst part was having to face my father. That was pretty much a low point in my life.

It was also a catalyst. Because of that experience I said, "*Never again* will I rely on someone else to take care of my money for me. If I lose it, so be it, but I have to be responsible for my own financial well-being."

So I started learning about money, and I started experimenting with investments. Sometimes I was successful; other times I was not. But what I found out was that the more I learned, the more I made. The more I learned, the more control I had. Instead of feeling hopeless and helpless when it came to money, I began to feel I had power over my own financial situation. I was becoming accountable, and it was the best feeling in the whole world.

Today, 12 years later, my situation is dramatically different. Not only am I a good steward of my own money but I also teach others how to do the same.

People often ask me why I feel so compelled to share my story, and what I learned as a result of it, with others. Why not just apply what I learned to my own life and be done with it? . . . And everyone lived happily ever after. The end.

First, my story points to the moral that if it can happen to a smart, young, up-and-coming business executive, imagine how most people must struggle with personal finance. But more importantly, I am proof that no matter how poorly you have handled money in the past, you can make a conscious decision to change it—and succeed.

Second, I believe that if you are really lucky, you will always learn from your mistakes. If you are truly blessed, you have the opportunity to take what you have learned the hard way and use it to help others. In fact, I believe there is a moral imperative to do so.

Third, the need for financial education today is reaching crisis levels. Studies indicate that our financial literacy isn't keeping pace with the demands being put on us. This is especially true of women, minorities, young people, and the less educated.

But the problem is certainly not limited to those groups. In fact, those I would expect to score highest in financial literacy—near retirees who have presumably made a great number of financial decisions during their lifetime—don't understand basic concepts necessary to make sound financial decisions. They, too, are in desperate need of financial education.

In a 2004 study, early baby boomers aged 51 to 56 were asked the following questions: "If the chance of getting a disease is 10 percent, how many people out of 1,000 would be expected to get the disease?" and "If five people all have the winning number in the lottery and the prize is $2 million, how much will each of them get?" Anyone who answered either of the first two questions correctly was asked a third question: "Let's say you have $200 in a savings account. The account earns 10 percent interest per year. How much would you have in the account at the end of two years?" Eighty percent of the participants were able to correctly determine that 10 percent of 1,000 is 100. Merely 50 percent could divide 2 million by five to get the lottery question right. Only 18 percent could compute the compound return over two years in the third question.[1]

A 2003 Washington State University study found very little understanding of financial instruments among the general population. Most people had no idea that bond prices fall as interest rates rise, for example. Many did not know what a no-load mutual fund was, or that mutual funds do not pay a guaranteed rate of return. More than one-third did not know that stocks had returned more than bonds over the last forty years, and many did not know about the basic concept of diversification to spread risk.[2]

The Organisation for Economic Co-operation and Development defines financial education as, "The process by which financial consumers/investors improve their understanding of financial products and concepts and, through information, instruction, and/or objective advice, develop the skills and confidence to become more aware of financial risks and opportunities to make informed choices, to know where to go for help, and to take other effective actions to improve their financial well-being."[3] Research has established a clear link between those who understand things like simple percentage calculations and compound interest and those who save and plan for retirement. There is a clear link between financial education and economic behavior. When viewed in those terms, can there be too many voices? If my story encourages just one person to put his/her financial house in order, then the story is worth telling.

Maybe you are single and really need to do a better job with your finances. Maybe you are married and want to be able to participate with your spouse in financial matters on more equal footing. Maybe you are after a safety net, just in case. Or maybe you want or need to become a full-fledged family CFO.

Unfortunately, we are a little bit like the proverbial soul who died of thirst in the middle of the ocean. Thanks to the Internet, financial information is all around us, but there is too much of it, it is not in a very usable form, and some of it can be downright harmful.

My purpose in writing this book is to give you a simple, straightforward guide to the basics of personal finance, based on my personal and professional experience, with the ultimate goal of your achieving financial success. My definition of financial success is being able to do what you want, when you want, without worrying about how to pay for it.

I believe financial success requires four things: to plan prudently, to save prodigiously, to invest wisely, and to manage risk. This is not earth-shattering news. These things are simple. They are doable. But they are obviously not easy; otherwise, we would all be millionaires, and I wouldn't have lost all of that money.

Financial success starts with a simple principle. If you earn $100 and spend $110, you will always be poor—it doesn't matter how much money you earn. If you earn $100 and spend $90, you will always have money—it doesn't matter how little you earn. If you want to be financially successful, you must *spend less than you earn.*

Once you have put away enough money to cover emergencies, start to invest your savings. The key to investing wisely is knowledge. I believe a financial education is one of the best investments you can possibly make. Sadly, you probably didn't get it in school, and you more than likely didn't get it from your parents either. It is up to you to fill in that gap in your education.

Investing is simply a trade-off between risk and reward. You cannot have one without the other. That law is as fundamental as gravity—it cannot be suspended. The investor who manages that trade-off well will do well. If you don't, you won't. Too much risk—or too little—can be equally detrimental to achieving financial success. Your job is to always maintain a happy medium.

Risk is connected with financial success in many ways. For example, more than 66.7 percent of high-net-worth individuals in the United States are entrepreneurs,[4] even though only 11 percent of the general population are entrepreneurs.[5] That makes sense, given that profit is the reward for risk. The entrepreneur takes the risk to start and sustain a business and therefore makes more, when successful, than the person who works for someone else and has less risk. But he/she also stands to lose more if the business fails, which it often does.

The good news is that you don't have to be an entrepreneur to be financially successful; you just have to act like one. Most successful entrepreneurs I know have three traits you need in order to be financially successful: determination, self-reliance, and self-confidence. People sometimes ask me how I went from being broke to not being broke in 12 years. I tell them I decided to. That is the truth. Without commitment and determination, you probably won't get there because financial success requires making hard choices. Usually that means giving up what you want now for the opportunity to have something better down the road. That is hard, I know.

Here are some other things most people find difficult: not getting caught up in what everyone else is doing, and not doing the same thing over and over yet expecting a different result. For example, when the traditional Wall Street offerings didn't meet my objectives, I created my own. If what you're doing isn't working, change what you're doing. Seems obvious, doesn't it?

Half of Americans don't believe they can create a secure retirement.[6] Sadly, they are right, because if you don't believe you will, then you most assuredly won't.

Why do so many people doubt their ability to achieve financial success? Is it because they are afraid to try? Is it because they've been told they can't do it? Is it because we are a gluttonous, consumer goods–oriented society in which no one knows the value of delayed gratification anymore?

Maybe.

But maybe, just maybe, it is because we do not believe we deserve financial success. One thing I know for sure, anything I believe I am unworthy of—love, money, respect, friendship—will elude me until I can say with certainty, "I deserve this!"

Do you deserve financial success? Is that what you want for you and your family? If so, let's create an action plan for you to achieve it.

SECTION ONE

Be the Family CFO

chapter 1

WHAT IS A FAMILY CFO?

A man, to carry on a successful business, must have imagination.
He must see things as in a vision, a dream of the whole thing.
—Charles M. Schwab

DID YOU KNOW THAT there are many similarities between managing a successful business and managing your personal finances? Yet you don't have to have years of management experience to profit from this way of thinking. You just need to borrow a few of the basic principles.

So let's meet a typical family CFO. Got a mirror handy? It's you!

If you are reading this book, chances are *you* are your family's CFO, whether you have thought of it in those terms or not. If you pay the bills, balance the checkbook, decide (or want to) where to invest your money, and figure out (or want to) where to get the money to meet your life's objectives, then you are the family CFO.

That's an awesome responsibility. In essence, that makes you responsible for the financial health of a fairly big organization. Just look at the cash flows of your family, or your personal cash flows if you are single. Add them up and you would probably be surprised at how significant they are.

So, if you really are the family CFO, don't you think it's time to start acting like one? After all, if you're going to do the job, you might as well do it with intention, right?

Your job as family CFO can be described by three activities: planning, managing assets and liabilities, and managing behavior. We'll look at each activity separately and then we'll see how each is applied to the four building blocks of financial success—plan prudently, save prodigiously, invest wisely, and manage risk.

Time management expert Alan Lakein is famous for saying, "Failing to plan is planning to fail." He defines planning as "bringing the future into the present so that you can do something about it now."

Every successful business, including the business of personal finance, needs a plan at a high level. In my company, I have a one-page strategic plan that covers everything from our quarterly objectives to our "Big Hairy Audacious Goal" (a term Jim Collins and Jerry Porras coined in their July 2006 *Harvard Business Review* article titled "Building Your Company's Vision") that may take ten years or longer to realize.

A supersize version of our plan hangs on a wall where every single employee can see it. As a company, we manage to that plan. In fact, we have a ten-minute all-employee huddle *every day* to make sure we stay focused and on plan.

Our big goals aren't focused on money. They revolve around fulfilling our purpose. Money is just a way of keeping score.

Your financial goals are probably not only about the money either; they're about the joys in life that financial security can bring. You must be absolutely clear about what you want to accomplish, when, and why if you expect to be financially successful.

Goals determine what you're going to be.

—Julius Erving

In addition to goal setting, a family CFO should do planning activities on a regular basis. These might include budgeting, quantifying goals, identifying and managing risks, and tax and estate planning.

It is not enough to plan once and then expect the plan to magically happen. Most plans have to be revisited on a periodic basis. You must revise your plan in meaningful ways as your circumstances change.

Plans are road maps, but they aren't carved in stone. Sometimes, despite all the preplanning, you just have to invent your way to the top. Again, if what you're doing isn't working, change what you're doing.

For the purposes of this book, I include the reporting function within planning. Forward-looking plans are much more realistic when we know what has happened in the past. Plus, when we periodically revisit our plan to make adjustments, we need some sort of reporting mechanism to know whether or not our plan is working. How we are doing against plan will tell us if the plan needs to be revised.

I also include knowledge gathering as part of planning, even though I am tempted to break it out into its own activity. In fact, I would say the first step to becoming a capable family CFO is a commitment to lifelong learning.

Now, I know that right here I am in danger of losing you. Some of you are tempted already to put this book down. You're thinking, "I don't have time to learn all there is to know about personal finance and investing. I would rather pay someone to do it so I don't have to learn this stuff. Please, just tell me what to do."

Sorry, it doesn't work that way.

A prince who will not undergo the difficulty of
understanding must undergo the danger of trusting.
—Lord Halifax

Financial success requires critical thinking. It would be nice to think a broker, an insurance agent, or a financial planner was capable of that, but they aren't. Not as long as they are paid a commission for selling you products.

Think about it. I am an advisor and I have two funds to sell. Company A (a low-cost index fund) has gotten exactly the same return as the market year after year for the last ten years. Company B (an expensive, actively managed fund) has under-performed Company A's fund by 2 percent year after year. All things being equal, which fund am I going to sell to my client?

But all things aren't equal, are they? After all, people are buying Company B's fund. In fact, under-performing, actively managed funds outsell index funds by more than five to one![7]

The reason is the huge financial incentive for Mr. Financial Advisor (not you the investor) to sell Company B's fund. Otherwise, who in their right mind would ever buy it? On the other hand, Mr. Financial Advisor gets little or no commission for selling an index fund—hence, the 5-to-1 ratio.

An investment in knowledge always pays the best interest.
—Benjamin Franklin

Financial education is your best weapon against being taken advantage of. Think of it as being a big, mean-looking dog in your yard. If I'm a burglar, I'm probably going to go rob someone else's house. Why work that hard?

That is exactly what financial education does for you. A little goes a long way because plenty of people are blissfully ignorant of how the system really works. As long as you know more than they do, chances are Wall Street will get rich off them instead of you.

To recap, then, the planning activity represents three things: (1) bringing the future into focus so we can affect it; (2) reporting on the past so we know how we are doing; and (3) gathering outside knowledge so we can make good decisions.

Planning is largely an intellectual activity. The second activity of the family CFO, managing assets and liabilities, is a very hands-on function. The planning function determines, in advance, how you will balance the present with the future. The management function is where you put those plans into action.

It is better to do the wrong thing than to do nothing.
—Winston Churchill

I take a narrow view of assets. While it could be argued that an asset is anything that has value, I define an asset as anything you own that has the potential to appreciate in value.

Using this definition, a car, for example, is not an asset, unless you happen to own a 1939 Lagonda V-12. Your clothes, your furniture, and your plasma television are not assets either. They are paraphernalia.

Your stock portfolio, savings account, equity in your home, 401(k), individual retirement account (IRA), real estate, or business, on the other hand, are all assets. These are the things the family CFO must manage.

Liabilities are anything you owe to someone else. Your mortgage, car loans, leases, credit card debts, student loans, and lines of credit are all examples of liabilities.

The difference between your assets and your liabilities is your net worth. Your net worth can be further divided into liquid net worth and total net worth.

Liquid net worth is that portion that is readily available. In the list of assets above, your savings account would be considered the most liquid, followed by the stock portfolio. The business, real estate, and home equity items are illiquid. IRA and 401(k) monies are in between, depending on your age.

Your liquid net worth would be the sum of your liquid assets minus short-term liabilities. Your total net worth is the sum of all your assets minus all your liabilities.

When it comes to managing assets and liabilities, the job of the family CFO is to get maximum benefit from them over your entire lifetime. This is what economists refer to as maximizing utility. Of course, this is not a purely mathematical equation because different people will view benefit differently based on what is important to them.

That brings us to the hardest activity of the family CFO: managing the behaviors that diminish your chances of achieving the financial success you deserve.

Have you ever noticed how easy it is to know what you should do with your money but how hard it is to actually do it? That is because our relationship with money is very complex. Our financial behavior is affected by a tangled web of psychological, sociological, and physiological pressures. Let me give you a personal example.

At one point in my life, I was an options trader. I had three mentors who taught me how to be successful as a trader. What they taught me about trading also influences the way I invest and how I teach others to invest. (Note: Trading and investing *are not* the same thing. Trading is hunting. Investing is farming.)

One of those mentors was a psychologist who had spent much of his career working for hedge funds, specialist companies, and the proprietary trading desks of the big Wall Street firms. Specifically, he counseled their traders on how to control their behavior. This is not dissimilar to the function of a sports psychologist or professionals who specialize in the psychology of performance.

Of course, today we have the recognized fields of behavioral finance, neuroeconomics, and socionomics. But up until recently, if these areas of study existed, they did not have a name. Even today, many people don't realize that some psychologists specialize in this area; most of us are only vaguely aware of the behavioral aspects of financial success.

The one absolute requirement of a money manager is
emotional maturity. If you don't know who you are,
the stock market is an expensive place to find out.

—Adam Smith

One of the first things the organizational psychologist said to me when we started working together was, "Whatever issues you have will play themselves out in your trading."

My immediate reaction was: "What issues? I don't have any issues. What kind of psychobabble is this? I want to learn how to trade, not be psychoanalyzed!" It was years later before I would allow myself to see that he was right. Boy, did I have issues!

Not only that, I eventually realized that what he said doesn't apply just to trading. It applies to all aspects of money. There is a reason why money issues are among the most frequently cited causes for divorce.

Behaviors that are detrimental to financial success include: (1) living beyond your means; (2) not saving for the future; (3) taking unnecessary risk; (4) relying on others to make important financial decisions for you; and (5) being uninformed. It's pretty easy to see how all of these behaviors can be by-products of such issues as self-esteem, self-control, approval seeking, and caretaking, among others.

Each of us has a story that dictates how we deal with money. Some of us are fortunate enough to have a story that makes us good with money. Most of us, though, are not so lucky. Look at your story and the behaviors that result. Then start managing those behaviors to achieve the result you have planned for.

What is your relationship to money? Do you avoid it? Are you angry at it? Are you afraid of it? Do you fight with it? Or do you respect it?

To manage your behavior, you have to understand the subconscious motivations behind your actions and change them.

chapter 2

WHY SHOULD I BECOME A CAPABLE FAMILY CFO?

The highest use of capital is not to make more money,
but to make money do more for the betterment of life.
—Henry Ford

IF MONEY WERE NO object, what would you like to be doing? Take a moment to think about this before you read any further.

What did you come up with? What is important to you? Family? Friends? Travel? Sending your kids to great schools? Not having to go to work every day? Getting really good at your favorite sport? Making the world a better place in some way?

Whatever your answer, that is the place you are trying to get to. That is your goal. Whether or not you get there depends on one thing, and one thing only: the choices you make from here on out. The only difference between the life you live today and the life you will be living five years from now is the choices you will make in the meantime.

This is the principle of accountability, and I believe it is fundamental to financial success. You are solely responsible for whatever situation you find yourself in. If you don't like the situation, you can look back and see the choices you—no one else—made that got you there.

Just as a side note, you can also look back and clearly see the choices you made that helped you build the life that you now love. If you are not there yet, take a moment to imagine how that would feel.

So, your circumstances are the direct result of your choices. In this day and age, the financial choices you have to make are becoming ever more complex. The consequences, too, are much more extreme. And the role models for success are becoming harder and harder to find.

Our grandparents kept most of the money they saved in a passbook savings account. As late as 1983, less than 20 percent of American households owned common stock.[8] Many working Americans had employer or military pensions and lifetime healthcare benefits. Insurance was pretty straightforward; just like the State Farm logo says, it covered life, health, and automobiles. When you dealt with your local banker or insurance agent, he was a friend and neighbor, a pillar of the community.

Today, of course, things are different. We have a lot more to manage. Name any one area of personal finance and think about the myriad choices we now have.

SAVING. Do I use a brick-and-mortar bank or an Internet bank? Do I choose a community bank or a behemoth? Are they going to give me free checking, and if so, is it really free? Should I write a check for my bills, use a credit card, a debit card, or an online bill-pay? Do I put my money in an interest-bearing checking account, a savings account, a CD, or a money market fund?

MORTGAGES. Do I go to my bank, a mortgage broker, or an Internet site like LendingTree? What kind of loan should I take (I can count ten different types other than the traditional 30-year fixed)?

INVESTING. Discount brokerage firms were born on May 1, 1975, as a result of a law that required brokerage firms to do away with fixed pricing and to negotiate commissions with individual customers. Among the large number of discount brokerage firms, many of which are online, are Charles Schwab, Fidelity Investments, E*Trade, TD Ameritrade, optionsXpress,* and Scottrade.

Prior to the Internet, access to markets and information was very limited. Today, investors can choose between self-directing their investments and paying someone to do it for them. Our grandparents had one choice—a broker. We have financial advisors of all stripes and colors: brokers, financial planners, certified financial planners, and financial education companies. Even banks, insurance agents, and CPAs are now getting into the act.

And what about the investment choices that have proliferated in the last few years? A portfolio no longer consists of a simple allocation between stocks and bonds. Now we have actively managed funds, index funds, fundamentally indexed funds, closed-end funds, REITs, exchange traded funds, fixed annuities, variable annuities, hedge funds, currencies, commodities, options, and futures to choose from.

TAXES. The U.S. Tax Code currently consists of 3.4 million words. If we printed it at 60 lines per page, it would be more than 7,500 pages long![9] Need we say more?

ESTATE PLANNING. My husband, Jim, and I just finished our estate plan. As these things go, ours is very simple. We have no kids. We want to make sure our animals are taken care of and then leave everything else to charity. Yet, you'd be surprised at all the decisions we had to make.

For instance, what is the effect of community property versus property we each brought to the marriage? How do our beneficiaries get full value from our business? Should we have a family member as executor

---

*See the appendix for disclosure information regarding optionsXpress.

or a paid executor? How do we make sure the trustee handles our assets the way we intended? If Jim died before me, should I discontinue the life insurance? It goes on and on.

Risk comes from not knowing what you are doing.
—Warren Buffett

If the decisions we make in any of these areas are uninformed, we stand a very real chance of suffering far-reaching negative consequences. A paper published by the Center for Retirement Research at Boston University says 90 percent of married adults aged 51 to 61 will experience a financially disruptive event—or be married to someone who does—over any ten-year period.[10] The prevalence of the events increases with age, but the odds are still pretty high even for a young person.

The degree to which these events—which include loss of a job, onset of a disability, death of a spouse, caring for an aging family member, and many others—disrupt your current and future standard of living is directly proportionate to the quality of financial decisions you've made up until that point. Simply put, better decisions yield better results.

One-third of all employer-sponsored pension plans were closed or frozen between 2005 and 2007.[11] Healthcare benefits to retirees are also declining rapidly. And then there is Social Security and Medicare.

Some people choose to ignore the possibility that Social Security and Medicare will fail before the last baby boomers retire. The son of one of my students asked, "What is the government going to do? Let 76 million baby boomers starve?" If you want to gamble on the kindness of strangers, or the financial backing of the government, then becoming a capable family CFO is probably not going to be a priority for you.

But if you believe, as I do, that (1) you are accountable for your situation, today and tomorrow; (2) your decisions will determine that situation; and (3) better decision making leads to better results, then you have every reason in the world to invest the minimal time and effort it requires to take control of your financial future and become a competent, confident family CFO.

SECTION TWO

Plan Prudently

chapter 3

CREATE PERSONAL FINANCIAL STATEMENTS

Money is a kind of poetry.
—Wallace Stevens

ON MY JOURNEY FROM riches to rags to riches, one area of concentration that helped me create financial success was to think like an entrepreneur.

When my husband and I first started our business, we spent almost all of our time trying to drum up clients and provide them with top-notch service. You wouldn't think there would be much to account for in such a small two-person firm, but you'd be surprised.

One of the things I had learned from an earlier business failure was to always keep a close eye on the money. That way, you'll never be surprised. From day one, I used software to track our bank accounts, credit cards, receipts, expenses, and so forth.

At first I didn't bother too much with financial statements for the business because just eyeballing the checking account balance gave me a pretty good idea where we were. But, as the business grew, my system had to become a little more sophisticated.

Soon I had to start projecting future expenses and future revenue in a cash flow projection so that I didn't spend money in the present that I was going to need to meet future liabilities. I had to put money aside—in what I thought of as buckets—so it was available when I needed it.

Eventually, we graduated to full-fledged financial statements. For one thing, we needed to know how we had done in the past in order to project the future. For another, others wanted to know how we had done before they would extend us credit.

To drift is to be in hell, to be in heaven is to steer.

—George Bernard Shaw

Today, our key financials—past, present, and future—hang on an office wall, as part of our strategic plan, for everyone to see. If you don't know what has happened in the past and you can't visualize the future, what chance do you have of arriving where you want to go?

I've never been big on letting hope and luck take care of things for me. Each of us floats down the financial river of life. We can either be like a leaf, subject to the whims of the current, or we can chart our own course. Financial statements are the map that tells you where you've been, where you are, and how to get where you're going.

If you come to a fork in the road, take it.

—Yogi Berra

My husband and I also have a set of personal financial statements, separate from the business. I started mine when I determined to really get my life together. I had goals in eight different areas of my life. One of those areas was personal finances.

I am not a paper person. If a document is important, I scan it. But I still have those worksheets I created many years ago. I just can't throw them away. They are a reminder of where I have been, how far I have come, and the road I traveled to get here.

I pulled them out when I started writing this section. Do you want to know what my financial goals were way back then? There were five:

1. Build a net worth equal to (my age times my annual income) ÷ 10. (This formula comes from Thomas Stanley's *The Millionaire Next Door*, a very influential book in my life.)
2. Create passive income that exceeds my monthly living expenses.
3. Minimize taxation as a percentage of income and net worth.
4. Reduce expenses as a percentage of taxable income.
5. Zero debt excluding mortgage.

Now I have different goals, of course, but this is where I started. And they were pretty lofty goals at the time, considering that I had no money and I was deeply in debt!

You can see by looking at the goals I outlined for myself that there was no way to know if I was making progress if I didn't have some kind of personal financial statements. Net worth comes from a personal balance sheet. Annual income comes from a personal income statement. Without knowing what my expenses were as a percentage of my income in the past, how could I know if that percentage was declining or what I had to do to make that percentage decline?

If you don't know where you are going, you might wind up someplace else.

—Yogi Berra

So let's take a more detailed look at personal financial statements and how you can create your own. The easiest way is to track all of your financial affairs in a software program, like Intuit's Quicken or Microsoft Money. As long as you put in the work on the front end, either of these programs will print reports galore at the click of a mouse.

If you are a person who finds a software program too structured, create your own system. For example, you might use Microsoft Excel to track your expenses and create reports.

Whether you use financial software, an Excel spreadsheet, or a pad of paper and a calculator doesn't matter. The key point is to create your personal financial statements, update them regularly, and share them with your "management team."

Jim and I don't have daily huddles like we do in the business, but we do sit down together regularly—usually about once a quarter—to discuss our personal financials. That way we both know exactly where we stand against our goals, and we can make adjustments when necessary.

Your personal financial statements should consist of an income statement and a balance sheet. An income statement shows where your money comes from, what it gets spent on, and how much is being saved. A personal balance sheet compares assets to liabilities to determine your net worth. Net worth is the ultimate measure of financial success. Your goal is to consistently increase your net worth.

Figures 1.1 and 1.2 show samples of a personal income statement and a personal balance sheet. (You can download an Excel workbook containing these samples from our Web site at howtobethefamilycfo.com.)

FIGURE 1.1

PERSONAL INCOME STATEMENT FOR JOE AND SALLY SMITH AS OF APRIL 15, 20XX			
	Last Year	**YTD**	**YTD Projected**
Income			
Earned Income			
Net Job or Self-Employment (Joe)	$85,125	$23,409	$70,675
Net Job or Self-Employment (Sally)	$76,342	$20,994	$63,250
EARNED INCOME SUBTOTAL	**$161,467**	**$44,403**	**$133,925**
Passive/Portfolio Income			
Real Estate (Net Profit)	—	—	—
Business (Net Profit)	—	—	—
Royalties	—	—	—
Interest	$23	$16	—
Dividends	$109	$45	—
Realized Capital Gains (excludes retirement accounts)	$8,734	$1,245	$3,575
PASSIVE INCOME SUBTOTAL	**$8,866**	**$1,306**	**$3,375**
TOTAL INCOME	**$170,333**	**$45,709**	**$137,500**
Expenses			
Essentials			
Rent or Mortgage	$14,760	$4,059	$12,100
Grocery	$9,360	$2,652	$7,975
Transportation	$4,744	$1,423	$4,125
Medical and Dental	$247	$286	$825
Childcare	$20,800	$5,720	$17,050
Insurance	$5,856	$1,610	$4,675
Retirement Plan Contributions	$22,000	$6,050	$18,150
Taxes	$15,984	$4,662	$14,025
ESSENTIALS SUBTOTAL	**$93,751**	**$26,462**	**$78,925**

continued on page 32

continued from page 31

PERSONAL INCOME STATEMENT FOR JOE AND SALLY SMITH AS OF APRIL 15, 20XX			
	Last Year	YTD	YTD Projected
Discretionary			
Clothing	$4,178	$1,253	$3,575
Eating Out	$7,420	$2,226	$6,600
Entertainment	$4,765	$1,429	$4,125
Recreation	$540	$162	$275
Vacation	$6,952	$2,085	$6,050
Personal Services	$17,475	$5,242	$15,675
Other	$7,672	$2,301	$6,875
DISCRETIONARY SUBTOTAL	**$49,002**	**$14,698**	**$43,175**
TOTAL EXPENSES	**$142,753**	**$41,160**	**$122,100**
NET CASH FLOW	**$27,579**	**$4,549**	**$15,400**

FIGURE 1.2

PERSONAL BALANCE SHEET AS OF APRIL 15, 20XX			
	Two Years Ago	**Last Year**	**Current Year**
Assets			
Checking Account	$10,234	$12,485	$15,231
Savings Account	$65,000	$65,000	$65,000
Pension	—	—	—
Company Stock or Options	—	—	—
Taxable Brokerage Account	$213,300	$232,497	$253,421
Joe's Traditional IRA	$87,453	$95,323	$103,902
Sally's Traditional IRA	$64,532	$70,339	$76,669
Joe's Roth IRA	$2,765	$3,013	$3,284
Sally's Roth IRA	—	—	—
Income Producing Real Estate (Net)	—	—	—
Home Equity	$54,973	$52,759	$53,814
Other Real Estate	—	—	—
Business Value (Net)	—	—	—
Collectibles	—	—	—
Cash Value of Insurance Policies	—	—	—
ASSETS SUBTOTAL	**$498,257**	**$531,416**	**$571,321**
Equity in Vehicles	$16,742	$4,298	$5,498
Other Personal Property	$20,000	$20,000	$20,000
PARAPHERNALIA SUBTOTAL	**$36,742**	**$24,298**	**$25,498**
TOTAL ASSETS	**$534,999**	**$555,714**	**$596,819**
Liabilities			
Credit Card Balances	$1,121	$2,113	$992
Car Loans	$34,234	$64,236	$63,237
Personal Loans	—	—	—
Mortgages	$219,034	$216,405	$213,808
Student Loans	—	—	—
Other Debt	—	—	—
TOTAL LIABILITIES	**$254,389**	**$282,754**	**$278,037**
REAL NET WORTH (EXCLUDING PARAPHERNALIA)	**$243,868**	**$248,662**	**$293,284**

The income statement subtracts expenses from income to determine your net savings. Income is divided into two sources: earned income and passive or portfolio income. Expenses are also divided into two categories: essentials and discretionary.

Most of us rely heavily on earned income. Earned income comes from your job. This is the amount reported on your W-2 each year. Earned income requires you to go to work every day to collect it. If you stop working, the income stops also.

Passive income is money that comes in whether you work or not. Passive income typically comes from one of three sources: a business, real estate, or royalties.

If you own a business that operates independently of you, that is passive business income. If, on the other hand, the business cannot operate independently of you, then I would put any income from the business in the earned income category, whether it is W-2 income or not. You'll see why in just a moment.

Another type of passive income is generated by rental property. If you own rental property, the net income, after all expenses, would go on the line for real estate on the personal income statement. I suggest you use net numbers here to make your income statement cleaner and because, I hope, if you own a business or rental property, you own them inside some sort of entity, like an LLC or S Corp. That entity would have its own set of books to determine the health of the business. For purposes of your own personal income statement, however, just use the net income from business ventures.

The final form of passive income is royalties. These are not nearly as common as business or real estate income. Royalties are payments made to you in return for the licensing of intellectual property, though they may also include the payments for licensing oil, gas, or other mineral rights.

If you are an author, for example, you may receive royalty payments from a publisher. Songwriters receive a royalty every time their song is played or performed. Any form of intellectual property may generate royalty payments when licensed. Because you get paid on an ongoing basis without doing anything, royalties are considered passive income.

Portfolio income is the realized profit on an investment in paper assets such as stocks, bonds, or CDs. Portfolio income also comes from three primary sources: interest, dividends, and realized capital gains.

Interest is the money paid to you as a result of lending your money to someone else. Bonds and CDs are the most common type of securities that generate an interest payment. Of course, interest goes the other way too. It can be an expense you pay in return for borrowing money. We'll get to that shortly.

Dividends are payments made by a company to its shareholders. For purposes of your personal income statement, I am assuming all dividends are coming from ownership in shares of publicly traded companies or companies in which you do not own a controlling interest. Any dividends paid by your company would be included as passive income on the line for business income.

Realized capital gains are the profit on the sale of an asset. This could be profit from the sale of a stock or an option. It could also be the profit on the sale of real estate or your business.

You may have multiple forms of income from the same asset. For example, you may own a piece of rental property on which you receive rent. When you sell it, if you do so at a profit, there will be a one-time realized capital gain. If you own a business, it may generate earned income or, even better, passive income while you own it. When you sell it, if you do so at a profit, it will create a capital gain.

Of course, we aren't all lucky enough to sell everything at a profit. Sometimes we get caught in a declining market and may sell at a loss. Capital losses are a negative number on the capital gains line. In other words, it is subtracted from your capital gains and your total income in general.

To understand your financial situation, it is helpful to know how much of your income is earned and how much is passive. Earned income requires you to work at a job. Passive income is assumed to come on a regular basis without a great deal of effort on your part.

My definition of financial freedom is that position in life when you no longer have to work for a living. In other words, when your passive income exceeds your monthly expenses, you are financially free. I think that should be everyone's goal, from the time they start working onward. Armed with detailed information, you can take positive steps to turn your dreams into reality. Without it, you are financially adrift.

A final lesson we can take away from the company management, or entrepreneurial, model is that of responsibility and involvement. When a company succeeds, much of the credit goes to the CEO. When it fails, the CEO must likewise take full responsibility. No CEO can go very far by relying on expert advice that he/she doesn't understand and then blaming the experts when things don't go as planned.

A CEO must understand the basis for all decisions and take responsibility for them. Show me an absentee CEO and I will show you a company that is under-performing. The same is true in the business of your personal finances. To rely on someone else to make financial decisions on your behalf, without being fully aware of the implications and the logic behind them—whether that person is a spouse, a financial planner, a broker, or a mutual fund manager—is an incredible gamble.

Money is better than poverty, if only for financial reasons.
—Woody Allen

Letting others make financial decisions on your behalf may feel safe, but it is really quite dangerous. Financial security is one of our highest needs. Yet it is precisely this level of importance that often causes us to abdicate this responsibility to someone else. Fear of failing in this most critical area creates stress and uncertainty that we often deal with by not dealing with it.

Invest in your own personal development the same way a company invests in training for its key personnel. Get training. Read books. Stay away from people who only want to manage your money for you. Gravitate toward those who have a vested interest in teaching you how to take care of yourself and secure your own financial future.

The purpose of any business is to make money for its owners. The purpose of You, Inc.—that is, your personal finances—is not much different. In both cases, active hands-on, day-to-day involvement by management is required. Having a high-level objective, specific goals, a plan for attaining those goals, and detailed information from which you can monitor, track, budget, and plan will move you miles ahead on the path to financial freedom.

chapter 4

HAVE A PLAN, BUT DON'T OVERPLAN

A vision without a task is but a dream,
a task without a vision is drudgery,
a vision and a task
[are] the hope of the world.
—From a church in Sussex, England, c. 1730

HAVE YOU EVER KNOWN a successful company to operate without a plan? Without a budget? Without a vision? No.

All successful companies have a plan somewhere. It may be in the owner's head, or it may be the result of an expensive five-day off-site brainstorming session of the company's top management team, but there is always a plan. Why?

Think about the week before you left on your last vacation. What did you do? You wrote out a list to make sure you got everything done before you left. Have you ever noticed how much more productive you are right before you leave on vacation? That's because you have a very simple plan, your "To-Do List," and a deadline by which to complete your plan.

If no successful company can operate without a plan, and we know that having a plan makes us more productive and likely to achieve our goals, why do most of us go through life without one?

A personal plan turns meaningful goals and objectives in your life into smaller, more manageable pieces. A plan gives you more control over the direction your life takes. It gives you a basis from which you can evaluate all of your decisions. It gives you a better chance of achieving happiness and personal fulfillment.

Some people balk at the idea of a personal plan because they think it takes the spontaneity out of life. It can, if taken to an extreme, but a personal plan is not rigid. It should change over time because we change. Our goals and objectives change. The things that are important to us change. Our plan should change accordingly too.

Even if you're on the right track, you'll get run over if you just sit there.

—Will Rogers

Before I started writing this book, I read several books about . . . how to write a book! Dan Poynter's *Self-Publishing Manual,* which I found most helpful in this endeavor, said, "You are finished when the manuscript is 95% complete and 100% accurate. Don't wait for one more photo, one more statistic, or one more piece of information."[12]

The same is true of your plan. I am a big believer in the 80/20 rule, especially when it comes to planning. There is such a thing as too much planning. Why? Because as time passes, everything changes anyway.

Dwight D. Eisenhower said, "Plans are nothing; planning is everything." Military officers, like Eisenhower, undoubtedly create a very detailed battle plan before launching their troops into combat. The moment the first shot is fired, however, everything changes. Perhaps the enemy does something unexpected. Some hill that didn't initially seem important now needs to be taken. Resources suddenly become unavailable, or the other way around.

The value is not in the plan you create; the value is in the thinking that the process of planning forces you to do. To create a plan you must first decide what you are trying to accomplish. You have to do a gap analysis to figure out where you are falling short. You have to analyze all the resources available to you. Which are being utilized effectively? Which are not? What resources do you have that you hadn't considered?

Planning also forces you to look at contingencies. I happen to think that is one of the most useful aspects of creating a plan. You have to take a hard look at what might go wrong. It forces you to ask my favorite question, "What if . . ." All of this is far more useful than the actual plan itself, so don't go overboard on the plan.

The key to success is to keep growing in all areas of life—
mental, emotional, spiritual, as well as physical.

—Julius Erving

My own planning process started out strictly as a financial plan. That seemed to be the most immediate need and, quite frankly, required the least amount of introspection. After a year or so, my financial plan expanded to encompass my whole life. It still included my finances, but that became only one aspect of the plan. One of the things that is important to me—a core value, if you will—is to have a balanced life. Having a plan for one aspect of my life and not the others didn't feel very balanced to me. So I created a five-year plan that was wider in scope than just my personal finances.

Another reason to expand your financial plan into a life plan is that you need to know very clearly what you are doing all this for. No one should be saving and investing just for the sake of having a lot of money. You should be saving and investing for the things that being financially independent can give you. What those things are is different for everyone. Time to pursue your passion? More time with your family? A good education for your kids? Whatever it is, it should go beyond the mere making of money. The money is just one means of achieving an end that is important to you.

Each person's plan will be unique, and the way you create it will be too. Here is a little bit about my planning process. I hope it will help get you started on your own plan, in your own way.

In the previous chapter, I shared some of my financial goals from when I first started a formal personal planning process. I used the following sentences to stimulate my thinking as I began that process. (Unfortunately, it was so long ago, I can't remember their source, but I probably read them somewhere.)

1. Someday I'd like to . . .
2. I have always wanted to . . .
3. I'd really love to . . .
4. Wouldn't it be great if I could . . .
5. If it was a perfect world I would . . .

For each one of these, I came up with between five and ten answers. I know because I still have the piece of paper I wrote them down on. In fact, I am looking at it right now as I type this chapter.

Then I sat down and wrote out my dream in as much detail as I could. If I was living the life I really wanted, what would that look like?

What would I be like as a person? I tried to cover as many different aspects of my vision as I could.

Next, I listed obstacles, or what I preferred to call hurdles. I put them all down on paper. Finally, I started working on defining my specific objectives.

On a new piece of paper, I broke down my life into different categories. They were: Financial, W-2 Job, Business, Physical, Recreation, Lifestyle, Relationships, and Intellectual. Your categories may be different, depending on how you view your world.

Then I started listing specific goals for each category. Some categories had one goal; others had four or five. Each of these goals was tied back to what I had written when I filled in the blanks of the five open-ended sentences.

For example, one of my statements was, "I would really love to pay off all of my debts." Another one said, "I would really love to not feel like everything is such a struggle." One of the simplest devices I have ever heard for setting a goal came from a podcast interview of Kraig Kramers, former CEO of Snapper. He says, "Take a verb and a noun and a date and string them together and that's a goal."[13] Using the first of the five financial goals I listed in chapter 3, I would write, "Build a net worth equal to my age times my annual income divided by 10 by January 1, 2008." *Build* is the verb; *net worth* (loosely) is the noun; and obviously *January 1, 2008*, is the date.

Similarly, the fifth financial goal I listed—"Zero debt excluding mortgage"—wasn't constructed as a proper goal. Rewritten Kraig's way, that goal would read something like, "Pay off all debt, except for mortgage, by December 31, 2010."

Once I had written my goals for each category, I began to break them down individually. Each goal was transferred from my "Master Goal List" to its own planning worksheet. At the top of the worksheet, I rewrote the goal. Then I wrote out a list of the benefits of achieving that goal. For the benefit of zero debt I wrote, "Every dollar of unpaid interest expense is several additional dollars of net worth."

Further down the page I wrote, side-by-side, the obstacles (hurdles) to achieving that particular goal and any solutions I could think of. At the time, I was driving a 1992 Ford F350 pickup that had well over 100,000 miles on it. It was paid for, and I couldn't afford to buy something else if it died. As it turns out, that wasn't an issue. It now has about 170,000 miles and still runs, although I don't drive it more than maybe once a year!

Nevertheless, one of the hurdles I listed was, "Truck may break down before I have accumulated cash for a new vehicle." Another was, "I like material possessions." Toys are one of my weaknesses, and I have a tendency to want what I want when I want it. So I addressed both an external and an internal issue that needed to be brought forward to my conscious level if I wanted to achieve this goal. Number one, I had to take really good care of that truck, and number two, I had to be careful not to sabotage the plan by buying things that didn't move me toward my objectives. My solutions were to buy only used high-dollar items and to make shopping without buying a leisure time activity.

The next item I listed on each goals worksheet was the criteria I would use to measure success. Some of these were very lengthy and involved; others were very straightforward. The criteria for my goal of zero debt, for instance, read, "Any loans or unpaid credit card balances, legally owed, other than mortgage."

Think of the criteria as the definitions of any terms you use in your goal. Think of the process almost as if you were writing a contract—a contract with yourself. If one of your goals is to reduce expenses as a percentage of taxable income, then how are you going to define the words *reduce, expenses,* and *taxable income*? That is what goes in the criteria section.

Let me give you a very practical example. I defined *reduce* as "a quarter-over-quarter decline in expenses divided by taxable personal income." I had a much lengthier definition of *expenses*. I defined *taxable income* simply as "W-2 wages plus net profit from my business."

Some goals lend themselves to being quantified and displayed on graphs so that you can see your progress. Others are easier to track by milestones. The last section of each of my goals worksheets was what I called "Plan," but milestones is another way to think of it.

I listed as many specific milestones for each goal as I could, as well as a target date for meeting each milestone. I left a blank space beside each one for me to fill in with the date when it was actually completed. So, for example, one of my milestones was to pay off the mortgage on a piece of property I owned. Beside it, I had a target date for getting that done. Other milestones, related to other goals, included finding an accountant I enjoyed working with and taking a course in taxation.

The thing that impresses me most about America is the way parents obey their children.

—Duke of Windsor

At this point I would like to make a couple more observations about the planning process. First, you cannot create this plan in a vacuum if you are married or in a committed relationship. Think of you and your spouse as the senior management team of You, Inc. Both of you have to be brought into the plan if you hope to achieve it. You may or may not be able to deliver the plan to your minions—the children. Fortunately for Jim and me, our dogs do whatever we say.

Second, as I alluded to in the beginning of this chapter, things will change. The unexpected will happen and alter your life course. Things you thought were important will become unimportant over time, and the other way around. Priorities change and so will your plan.

Over the years, I have tried to maintain the following discipline: I sit down on at least a quarterly, sometimes a monthly, basis to look at how I am doing against my milestones. I love writing dates next to the items I have completed. I keep working at the ones I have missed. (Truth be told, some years I'm more disciplined at this than others. I find that the need tends to dictate the schedule.)

I don't make major revisions to my plan except once a year. It is my tradition, on New Year's Day, to sit down with my plan and completely rewrite it on fresh pieces of paper. I cross off the goals that have been achieved; that is, goals for which all milestones have been reached and dispensed with. I remove or modify goals that no longer apply and add new ones that have become priorities.

I want to encourage you to be honest with yourself and with each other as you go through this process. This plan is for no one but you. Be realistic about your shortcomings. Acknowledge them in your plan and write in ways you will work around them.

Finally, aim high. If you really want something, put it in the plan and figure out the steps to achieve it. Don't shortchange yourself or leave something out because some little voice inside your head says, "I could never do that." You can't if you don't try.

Don't wait. The time will never be just right.
—Napoleon Hill

Once you have your plan 95 percent complete and 100 percent accurate, as Poynter would say, get going. You'll be amazed at what you will accomplish. Your whole life will become as productive as the week before vacation.

chapter 5

PLAN NOW FOR THE INEVITABLE

No one can confidently say that he will still be living tomorrow.
—Euripides

WHO WANTS TO THINK about death, right? A lot of families, especially young families, put off estate planning. Maybe you think you don't have enough property or assets to justify an estate plan.

Think again. No matter what else you might have, if you have a kiddo under 18, you need an estate plan. Who would take care of your child(ren) if something happened to you? That is certainly not something you want a court to decide. You have life insurance, right? Let's assume your kids are the beneficiaries if something happens to you. When do they get control of that money? Who is going to manage it in the meantime? What is it to be used for?

Of course, we all hope and pray that this never becomes an issue. But hope as we may, bad things happen—even when people are young.

I had a friend in high school, for instance, whose mom had died when he was in grade school. When he was about 17, his dad died in a single-car accident, having fallen asleep at the wheel and wrapped his Corvette around a tree. The first thing my friend did with the insurance money he received was to buy himself his own Corvette! His dad could have ensured that the insurance money went for college or the down payment on a house had he thought ahead and put the proper provisions in his will.

WHAT IS ESTATE PLANNING?

Estate planning is the process of identifying and transferring all of your property after your death. Estate planning makes sure your estate is transferred according to your wishes and in accordance with any goals or objectives you might have.

Providing for minor children is generally at the top of the priority list for younger families. You might want to structure your estate plan so the maximum amount transfers to your beneficiaries and the minimum amount to Uncle Sam. That requires some preplanning. Another important aspect is making your wishes known and providing some structure in case you were to become incapacitated.

A common misconception is that estate planning is only for the rich and famous. Not true. It is your job to determine the disposition of anything you care about. That isn't always money.

For example, we have a writing desk that has been in my family since the late 1700s. It was brought over by ship from England. By tradition, it has been passed down from mother to first daughter in each family. I don't have any daughters, so the writing desk will go to my sister's oldest daughter—but only if I write it into my will. Otherwise, the disposition of the desk will be at the mercy of others who may or may not remember that those were my wishes.

CREATING AN ESTATE PLAN

So, exactly how do you go about creating an estate plan? Simply follow this ten-step process (each item is explained in full after the list):

1. **Develop objectives**
2. **Determine total assets and liabilities**
3. **Decide who gets what**
4. **Settle on an attorney, executor, trustee, guardians for the kids, and other agents**
5. **Figure out how much estate tax will be owed**
6. **Fill out a Designation of Beneficiary form for all retirement accounts and life insurance policies**
7. **Consider at least four documents**
8. **Sit down with your estate attorney**
9. **Create a What If . . . file**
10. **Communicate your wishes to others**

1. Develop objectives

When it comes to estate planning, I believe you should start with the end goal in mind. Therefore, the first step is to decide what you (or you and your spouse) want to accomplish through your estate plan. It usually works best if both of you think about this separately and then come together for a conversation about what is important to each of you.

Estate planning objectives customarily include, among others: (1) provide for the surviving spouse; (2) provide for a dependent family member; (3) name guardians or trustees for minor children; (4) provide for the education of minor children or grandchildren; (5) create a means of succession for a business; (6) provide a means of paying off debts, taxes, funeral expenses, and costs of settling the estate; (7) transfer specific property to specific people; (8) leave something to specific charities or organizations; (9) minimize estate costs and taxes; and (10) protect privacy by avoiding probate.

All of these and more might be objectives in your Estate Plan. Remember, there is no right or wrong answer, and there are many ways to achieve a given set of objectives. What matters is what is important to you. It's up to your estate attorney to come up with the best strategies for meeting your objectives. But he/she can't do the job unless you can state very clearly what you are trying to achieve.

2. Determine total assets and liabilities

In this step you will create some pretty detailed records about everything you own and everything you owe. Your personal financial statements from chapter 3 will be a good starting point.

Start with your assets. What are they? Where are they? How are they titled? Then go to your liabilities. Who do you owe, and how much? Your list should include everything on your personal balance sheet plus any life insurance policies. This is also a good time to make a detailed list of any personal belongings you might want to designate for specific people.

3. Decide who gets what

Some people may find this the hard part. Others of you will think it's easy. Again, I think this works best if you and your spouse both come up with your ideas separately and then discuss them together. Typically, each of you will have things that matter only to you, and they can sometimes slide through the cracks if you don't spend some time separately thinking about who gets what. This is particularly true with blended or extended families.

Once you each have your own ideas about how the property should be divided, and when, then you should have an honest conversation about any meaningful differences. Maybe your husband wants to leave $50,000 to his deadbeat brother who has never had a job and has always been mean to you. Now is the time to get that out on the table. Ideally, the two of you shouldn't be that far apart on these issues, but if you are, it's important to clear the air now.

4. Settle on an attorney, executor, trustee, guardians for the kids, and other agents

Now that you know what you are trying to achieve, what you have, and who is going to get your possessions, it is time to figure out who is going to carry out your wishes. First and foremost, this means choosing an estate attorney to help you formalize your plan. Beyond that, it may also include naming executors, trustees, guardians, and agents.

The best way to find an estate attorney is through word of mouth. Ask your friends, colleagues, relatives, and other advisors. If possible, get at least three recommendations and visit with each.

Ask them about their fees. Do they charge a flat fee or by the hour? Ask yourself how you would feel working with this person. Do they make you comfortable? Would your spouse or kids feel comfortable with them?

Once you decide on an attorney, he/she will need to know the persons you want to designate for the various other roles in your plan. At a minimum, you will need to decide on an executor, whose job is to make sure all your wishes are carried out and to manage the estate until it has been settled.

The executor shouldn't be chosen lightly. For one thing, it is no small job. Depending on the complexity of the estate, there is a long laundry list of things that must be done, and it can often take up to a year to settle an estate. Make sure the person is willing and able to do the job. Talk with both your primary and alternate choices before naming them in your will.

If your attorney recommends putting some or all of your assets in a trust, you will need to name a trustee. Similar to an executor, a trustee is responsible for protecting and managing all assets placed in the trust. A trustee is also responsible for making sure those assets are used to fulfill your wishes.

Trustees can be friends or family members. Sometimes they are attorneys or CPAs; sometimes they are professionals who work for a trust company. Who you choose will again depend on the complexity of the job you want them to do and the length of time you want them to do it for.

If you have minor children, you will want to nominate a guardian for them in your will. You cannot assume that the other parent will be alive or available to assume this responsibility. In the end, the court will decide on the guardian of your children if neither biological parent is alive. But the courts do put great weight on the express wishes of the parent and will generally accede to those wishes unless the person chosen as guardian is clearly unsuitable or does not wish to serve.

Finally, most estate attorneys will recommend that you have a Durable Power of Attorney document for medical issues and another one for financial issues. (These are discussed in more detail under item 7.) Each of these will require you to name an agent to act on your behalf in the event that you are incapacitated.

A related document is a Living Will, which spells out your wishes regarding the use of life-sustaining procedures. Without these documents, and an agent to act on your behalf, it might fall to the court to decide on both your medical and your financial affairs—something almost no one wants.

5. Figure out how much estate tax will be owed

If your estate in 2008 is worth more than $2 million, your heirs may have to pay estate tax. (The exclusion amount is $2 million in 2008, $3.5 million in 2009, and unlimited in 2010. In other words, no estate tax need be paid regardless of the worth of your estate if you die in

2010. Barring action from Congress to renew the law, it will expire, and the unified credit will revert to $1 million in 2011.[14]) It is important for you to know, in advance, a ballpark estimate of the estate tax. Otherwise, your heirs may be hit with a nasty surprise that could, potentially, wipe out the entire estate.

Imagine you and your spouse own a family business worth $6 million but few other liquid assets. If you both die, the business may have to be liquidated in order to pay the estate tax due. Illiquid assets that have to be sold in a hurry are often sold at deeply discounted prices. Years of work can be wiped out by the estate tax.

You can prevent this from happening, however, by making sure there are sufficient liquid assets in your estate to cover the tax bill. You can do that only by knowing how much estate tax will be due. Often, the best way to achieve the liquidity needed is with a life insurance policy.

The best way to ballpark the estate tax liability is by using one of the many estate tax calculators on the Internet. I have listed several of my favorites in the resources section at the back of this book. Searching the Internet using the term "estate tax calculator" will yield numerous others.

When determining the amount of estate tax liability, don't forget to consider state taxes. Not all states have estate taxes, but many do. The rates and exclusion amounts are different in each state. Again, the Internet is your best source to find out the specifics in your home state.

6. Fill out a Designation of Beneficiary form

Life insurance policies, IRAs, profit-sharing plans, pension plans, and other similar benefits plans are not controlled by your will. These accounts pass to your heirs according to the instructions contained in the Designation of Beneficiary form you last filled out for each of these accounts. It is very common for these documents to be either horribly outdated or missing altogether.

The younger you are, the more likely your Designation of Beneficiary forms need to be updated. I remember, for example, at one of my first jobs, the HR director shoved a Designation of Beneficiary form across the desk at me. Who was I going to leave my whopping $100 fortune in my 401(k) to? Many of us will list our parents, a sibling, or even a former boyfriend or girlfriend.

These forms need updating because the younger we are, the more our lives change. We find the love of our life, get married, settle down, and start a family. If something terrible happens, you sure don't want to wake up one day and realize a big hunk of your spouse's estate went to an old paramour or their ex by mistake!

Make a list of all the accounts you have which require a Designation of Beneficiary form. Every time you fill out one of these forms for the first time, add the account to your list. Add a column for the last time you checked and updated these forms and who you designated as the primary and contingent beneficiaries.

Make sure you keep these documents up to date. They are as important as a will, so fill them out with the same care and forethought. If you need to change a form, just request a new one from the company, fill it out, and send it back to them.

Finally, be sure to keep your list with all your other important papers. If you are really organized, attach a copy of each form to your list.

7. Consider at least four documents

There are four basic estate planning documents just about everyone should have. They are (1) a Testamentary Will; (2) a Living Will; (3) a Durable Power of Attorney for medical issues; and (4) a Durable Power of Attorney for financial issues.

A Testamentary Will spells out exactly what you want to have happen upon your death. It directs the transfer of assets, names an executor, and nominates someone to be the guardian of your minor child(ren). In the absence of a will, all of these things are left up to a court to decide. A will does not go into effect until you die and then only after it has been probated by a court.

A Living Will, also known as a Directive to Physicians or Advance Directive, tells physicians what actions you want them to take should you become permanently incapacitated. In other words, to what lengths should they go to sustain your life?

A related document is a Durable Power of Attorney for medical issues. The wording in it appoints someone to make medical decisions on your behalf should you become unable to do so. When choosing this person, think about the emotional nature of the decisions you might be asking him/her to make. I did not choose my husband or my mother in this capacity for that reason.

Finally, a Durable Power of Attorney for financial issues appoints someone to make financial decisions on your behalf when you are not legally able to do so. In this case, I did appoint my husband, with family members as backup.

These documents are the foundation of your estate plan. Still others may be required, depending on your objectives. Your estate attorney will guide you.

8. Sit down with your estate attorney

This is the stage where you give your attorney all the information he/she will need to create your estate plan. If you have been through all of the previous steps, this one should be pretty anticlimatic.

9. Create a What If . . . file

One of my clients (I wish I could remember which one to give proper credit, but I've forgotten) gave me the idea for a What If . . . file. A

What If . . . file is one that contains all of the things your spouse or others need to know about in case something happens to you.

Things to put in your What If . . . file should include (but are not limited to) the following:

1. Contacts—Include the names, addresses, and phone numbers for friends and family as well as contact information for doctors, lawyers, financial advisors, bankers, and accountants. In addition, there are other more run-of-the-mill contacts your spouse or executor might need, such as the housekeeper, the pool service, the yard service, the veterinarian, the teachers and coaches at your child's/children's school/schools.

2. Identification—Include such things as birth certificates, adoption papers, marriage certificate, passports, divorce papers, Social Security numbers, death certificates, military records, and immigration and naturalization records for each member of the family. Don't forget the pets. Does your dog or cat have a microchip? Put it in your What If . . . file.

3. Medical—Include immunization records, health history, prescriptions, health insurance coverage, and the phone number for each family member's primary care physician and any specialists.

4. Financial—The most important documents in this section include bank accounts, investment accounts, pensions, a list of credit cards with account numbers and phone numbers, a list of recurring monthly bills, real-estate transaction documents, deeds of trust, real estate title, mortgages and loan documents, car title and registration, business and partnership agreements, property tax statements, home improvement records, safe deposit box information, appraisals, household inventory, residential leases, vehicle leases, and more. Don't forget account login information for banks, brokerage firms, credit card companies, and online bill-pay services.

5. Insurance—Include documents for homeowners, renters, umbrella liability, earthquake, flood, hurricane and windstorm, and auto insurance policies. You should include not only copies of the policies themselves but also contact information for each insurance company and agent.

6. Estate planning—Include a Testamentary Will, trust documents, insurance policies, beneficiary designations, deeds to cemetery plots, and a Living Will. Again, make sure you include contact information for insurance companies, an estate attorney, a trust company, an executor, guardians, and trustees where appropriate.

The client who gave me this idea didn't stop there. She included things like what days the garbage was picked up, how much chlorine to put in the pool, and the oil-to-gas ratio for the lawnmower. She also included keys, data backups, and favorite family recipes.

You get the idea. She put in her file anything she did on a daily basis that someone else would need to do or know. You may not want to go into that much detail. But somewhere along the continuum of what is absolutely necessary and all the minutiae stored in your head is the right answer for you.

You should generally have multiple copies of all of your important documents. Consider who should have the signed original of each document. The signed original of your Testamentary Will, for example, should be in your files or kept by your attorney or both (which necessitates signing two). The original of a Living Will should be in the possession of your doctor or representative. Original documents concerning minor children should be given to the named guardian. You get the idea.

Then consider who should have copies. Who needs to know what is in those documents? Trusted family members, representatives, medical professionals, attorneys, trustees? Give them the necessary copies.

And finally, decide where and how to store your copies. You will want to keep your What If . . . file in a safe place that is also easily accessible. Some people like to put important papers in a safe deposit box to protect them from theft or damage. (Be aware that some state laws freeze or otherwise limit access to a safe deposit box after the owner's death. A key and power of attorney are not necessarily sufficient to guarantee immediate access. Therefore, consider carefully whether to store signed originals of your will and your deed to a burial plot[s] in a safe deposit box.) Other papers that you access regularly may be stored in a home safe or filing cabinet.

I recommend that in addition to these places, you have an emergency financial records kit that you can pick up and move at a moment's notice.

My parents and grandmother live in Durango, Colorado. On June 9, 2002, the Missionary Ridge forest fire broke out only a few miles from their home. "Over the next 40 days the fire consumed 72,962 acres, destroying 56 homes, 27 out buildings and burning 2,000–8,000 acres a day for the first week. The fire made significant advances, building massive ash-laden smoke columns which prompted the evacuation of 2,300 homes."[15]

When the order to evacuate their homes came, families were given only minutes to leave. My grandmother's home was one of those evacuated. It was saved only through the monumental efforts of family, friends, neighbors, and firefighters. Disasters like fires, floods, tornadoes, earthquakes, hurricanes, and even terrorist attacks can strike anywhere, anytime. In addition to your important records, consider keeping a set of keys; a couple of blank checks; an extra credit, debit, or ATM card; and even a stash of emergency cash on hand. That way, if you have to leave your house at a moment's notice, everything will be in one place and you can go right to it.

On the other hand, items like Social Security numbers, driver's license numbers, birth certificates, and bank account information are all that a thief needs to heist your identity. (In chapter 21, I go into the subject of identity theft in great detail.) If possible, store your emergency financial records kit in a secure location in your home so it is easy for you to grab and go to in a disaster but not for a thief to make off with if you are robbed.

10. Communicate your wishes to others

It's not just creating an Estate Plan that can be difficult. The more difficult thing is often talking about such a document. I think many adult children avoid talking with their parents about their estate because they don't want to appear to be greedy or insensitive.

The same thing happens with parents. They don't talk with their adult children in advance because they don't want to upset them or cause family friction.

That is all well and good, but this reluctance to speak or lack of foresight sometimes results in tragic unintended consequences. There are far too many horror stories of interfamily feuds breaking out over an inheritance or of the government inheriting the estates of people who died without a will. A good family CFO does not leave these things to chance.

DON'T LET IT RUST

I had my first will drawn up when I got my first job and began accumulating some small assets. I have to confess, years went by before I updated it. Not three years. Not five years. Not even ten years. I'm talking decades! A lot had changed over those years: the people who were in my life had changed, as had my financial situation—several times.

Any number of events should prompt you to revisit your Estate Plan.[16] Among those events are:

- Someone named in your estate plan has died.
- You have or adopt children.
- Your marital status has changed.
- State or federal tax laws have changed.
- Your relationship with a named attorney, executor, trustee, guardian, or agent has changed.
- Your child(ren) turned 18.
- The value of your estate has changed significantly.
- You acquire or dispose of a specific asset.
- You reach the age of 70½.
- Time has passed.

Review your plan every three to five years whether anything has changed or not.

Don't forget the pets

When you bring a pet into your home, you have accepted responsibility for its welfare just like for any other family member. Remember to make provisions for your pets should anything happen to you. Not only should you designate who will care for them but you should also consider providing for their care financially.

New laws have been passed in many states that formalize the right of an owner to set up a trust for benefit of their pets. When Jim and I completed our Estate Plan last year, the law was brand-new, and our attorney told us we were the first official "Pet Care Trust" he had done. So yes, you could say our animals are trust fund babies.

If you want a thing well done, do it yourself.

—Charles Spurgeon

The best thing to do is to decide what you want to have happen when you die, use the proper legal avenues to make sure that is exactly what will happen, and if possible, tell others of your plans and why.

You might be surprised. Having all those details buttoned down is just one less thing you have to worry about. Personally, I find it satisfying to know that if anything happens to me, all the details have been taken care of.

SECTION THREE

Save Prodigiously

chapter 6

CREATE A SIX-MONTH EMERGENCY FUND

After the ship has sunk, everyone knows how she might have been saved.

—Italian proverb

OVER THE YEARS, I have often received e-mails like this one:

> *I have very little money and I don't mean a couple of thousand either. I am lost in where to put it to make it grow and work for me. I tried to grow it but that doesn't seem to work. I don't seem to have a green thumb. How much do I save to even begin making my money work for me? I know I'm probably helpless, but I thought I would give it a shot. Thanks!*

The biggest mistakes I see people make are

1. Trying to invest before they save;
2. Trying to invest without really knowing what they are doing; and

3. Trying to turn almost nothing into a little something by taking too much risk, thereby almost guaranteeing that their nothing will always be nothing.

When you have no savings, your focus can't be on investing. The first thing you have to do is put at least six months of expenses in a savings account or money market fund. This is not negotiable. You should not be investing to try to create your emergency fund. You save that first!

WHAT IS AN EMERGENCY FUND FOR?

Consider an emergency fund sacrosanct. It is to be used solely for real emergencies. Your planning and budgeting should cover the small stuff, like when the dishwasher breaks or you need new tires for your car. Your emergency fund is for the really big stuff.

What kind of big stuff, you ask. A good rule of thumb is to tap your emergency fund *only* when your income is disrupted. This would include losing your job, you or a loved one being in a serious accident or becoming seriously ill—major financial upheavals.

Maybe you're thinking you don't need an emergency fund because such events will never happen to you. After you read the following e-mail from a student who completed one of our Snider Investment Method® workshops,* think again.

> *On June 9th my wife drove her motor scooter into the side of a moving furniture truck. She was airlifted to the hospital, and initially I was told she was not expected to live. She required a family member to be with her 24 hours a day in the hospital and also for post-hospital care. She was discharged from the hospital's rehabilitation unit on July 3rd, but still required*

---

* See the appendix for disclosures relating to the Snider Investment Method® and the Snider Investment Method Workshop.

24-hour care at home. She had follow-up surgery yesterday and is still in bed with 24-hour care required. Since we have little family near us that means me. She is expected to require full-time care for some time into the future, maybe another month or two.

I have my own business, and if I do not work, I do not get paid. Although I have not dipped into my [emergency] funds as yet, having that income there and available if I need it has allowed me to provide the care with an added financial peace of mind I would not have had otherwise. Most of her bills have not arrived, and I do not know to what extent I will need to utilize those funds. However, knowing that I have that [emergency fund] has allowed me to work only 6 days since June 9th.

As I mentioned in chapter 2, there is a 90 percent chance that a couple between the ages of 51 and 61 will experience a financially disruptive event over any ten-year period.[17] While the odds go down for younger age groups, they are nevertheless quite high and are getting higher by the day. Research shows that the incidence of financially disruptive events is increasing with each passing year. You must deal with far more uncertainty than your parents or grandparents did, which means you have to do more planning, and saving, up front.

HOW MUCH SHOULD BE IN MY EMERGENCY FUND?

Most experts will tell you that your emergency fund should be between three and six months of expenses. I know far too many people who lost their jobs between 2000 and 2003 and took a year or more to find a job to think that three months is enough. Six months of expenses is my number.

To figure out how much money that is, you have to first know how much you spend each month on necessities. If you had to, you could do without Starbucks for six months.

This is where the expense categories in the personal income statement we created in chapter 3 will come in handy. Remember that we broke expenses into two categories: essentials and discretionary. You want to take the average of your essentials over the last six months, multiply by six, and that is how much you should have in your emergency fund.

WHERE SHOULD I PUT IT?

The requirements for your emergency fund are that it must be liquid, it should be earning interest, and it should not be subject to any losses. Given these three requirements, your choices are either a savings account or a money market fund. You can't put the money into CDs because they are not liquid. In addition, you pay a penalty if you withdraw the money before the CD matures. You can't put the money in U.S. Treasury bonds because they can lose market value if you liquidate them before maturity.

Jim and I keep our emergency funds in an online bank because such banks often pay higher interest than brick-and-mortar banks do. We use the Orange Savings Account from ING Direct. There is no minimum deposit, no service charges, no fees, no penalties for withdrawal, and deposits are FDIC insured up to $100,000. (Note that this information was current as of March 3, 2008. We have had our savings with ING for a number of years but would certainly move it if a better option presented itself.)

Money market funds are a second option. Money market funds are mutual funds that invest in very short-term debt. If you have a taxable account at a brokerage firm, you can put your emergency funds in your brokerage account and use them to purchase a money market fund.

Money market funds have a net asset value of $1. If you buy 1,234 shares in a money market fund, for example, they will have a value of $1,234. The interest is paid separately and fluctuates depending on what the fund invests in. The yield on a money market fund is generally a little bit higher than from a savings account, but not always.

Most money market funds at brokerage firms give you check writing privileges. But remember, these funds are to be used *only* in the event of a true emergency.

chapter 7

KNOW THE DIFFERENCE BETWEEN GOOD DEBT AND BAD DEBT

A small debt produced a debtor; a large one, an enemy.
—Publilius Syrus

IS THERE SUCH A thing as good debt? Yes! The definition of good debt is money you borrow to buy an asset that appreciates in value— ideally at a faster rate than the interest rate on the loan. Two examples of good debt include the mortgage on your house and student loans. Presumably, the value of your house will rise over time provided you own it for long enough and didn't grossly overpay in the first place. And we know that an education increases our earning power significantly over our lifetime.

Bad debt is money you borrow to buy something that does not appreciate in value. Examples include a car loan, money to remodel your kitchen, and everything you buy with a credit card. If you want to be financially successful, banish bad debt.

Here are some fascinating facts about debt and credit cards:

- Approximately 851,000 U.S. households filed for bankruptcy in 2007, up 38 percent from 2006.[18]
- There were roughly 1.3 billion credit cards in use in the United States in 2004.[19] That number has undoubtedly grown.
- The original Diners Club card was issued in 1950 to let businessmen charge meals. It was pasteboard, with a list of the 27 restaurants that accepted it printed on the back. The first plastic card came out in 1955.[20] Today, there are about 20,000 different cards available in the United States.[21]
- Today's consumer is bombarded with between 3,500 and 5,000 marketing messages per day, compared to 500 to 2,000 in the 1970s.[22]
- About one-third of all purchases in the United States are made with some form of payment card—including credit, debit, and prepaid cards.[23]
- Total household debt in the United States, not counting mortgage debt, was about $2.46 trillion in 2007[24]—before World War II, most middle- and working-class families had no debt. Banks would not lend them money; they rented their home or paid for it as it was being built.
- A typical credit card purchase ends up costing 112 percent more than if cash were used.[25]
- A $1,000 charge on an average credit card will take almost 22 years to pay, and will cost more than $2,300 in interest ($3,300 total), if only 2-percent minimum payments are made.[26]

- About 40 percent of credit card accounts are paid off monthly—meaning 60 percent are not.[27]
- U.S. consumers used credit and debit cards to purchase an estimated $51 billion worth of fast food in 2006.[28]
- Average net worth of near retirees (household headed by someone between the ages of 55 and 64), including home equity: $248,700 in 2004.[29]
- The average interest rate on credit cards is 13.29 percent—the lowest in years.[30]
- Credit card companies took in $43 billion in late payment, over-limit, and balance transfer fees in 2004.[31]
- Nine of ten Americans claim credit card debt has never been a source of worry.[32]
- But 47 percent would refuse to tell a friend how much they owe.[33]
- Twenty-three percent of Americans admit to maxing out a credit card.[34]
- Eleven percent of Americans admit card debts went to collection.[35]
- Thirteen percent of Americans have been 30 days late paying credit card bills in the past year.[36]
- The average graduate student has $8, 216 in credit card debt.[37]
- The personal savings rate in the United States has dropped from 8 percent in the 1980s to zero in the fourth quarter of 2007.[38]
- Medical debts sink the ship in one of every 20 bankruptcies. Typical healthcare debt: $25,000. Typical victim: a senior on a fixed income. Typical scenario: pricey prescriptions bought on high-interest credit cards.[39]

After providing for your daily needs and establishing an emergency fund, getting rid of all bad debt is the most important thing you can do to guarantee a life free of financial stress.

HOW DO I GET OUT OF DEBT?

Several good books have been written on this topic. I like the *Automatic Millionaire* because the author, David Bach, gives you a system to follow rather than general advice. I know many people have also gotten excellent results with Dave Ramsey's *Financial Peace*. Both books are listed in the resources section at the back of this book. (Please be advised that although I disagree with both Bach and Ramsey when it comes to their advice about investing, I think their systems for helping people get out of debt are outstanding, which is why I recommend them.)

WHICH COMES FIRST, THE EMERGENCY FUND OR GETTING OUT OF DEBT?

If you don't already have an emergency fund and you are staring at a bunch of bad debt the answer to this question is you have to do both at the same time. If you were to work exclusively on creating your emergency fund, your credit situation would worsen dramatically, at double-digit interest rates, by the day. If you were to work exclusively on your debt situation and you lost your job before you cleared all your debt, all that hard work would go right down the drain because you had no emergency funds set aside.

I recommend that you alternate between the two. Calculate how much extra money you can set aside each month. In the first month, put it in your emergency fund. In the second month, use it to pay down bad debt. Third month, emergency fund; fourth month, debt payment. And so forth. Both of these areas are so important that I don't think you can afford to wait on either one. These are the foundation of financial success. Get them squared away as soon as possible.

SHOULD YOU PAY OFF
YOUR MORTGAGE EARLY?

The conventional wisdom used to be to pay off your mortgage as soon as you can. Retire with a paid-for home. Some personal finance writers still believe that. I used to believe it too, but not anymore.

Recent academic research says you may be making a big mistake if you are making accelerated mortgage payments and not contributing the maximum to tax-deferred retirement plans.

In particular, the authors of a study conducted by the Federal Reserve Bank of Chicago suggest that you are probably better off putting that money in your tax-deferred retirement accounts, like an IRA, a 401(k), or a 403(b), instead of paying down your mortgage. This is known as a tax arbitrage, meaning you take advantage of the difference between tax rates. The authors say the differential is between 11 and 17 cents on the dollar over the term of the mortgage, depending on the choice of investments you make inside the tax-deferred account.[40]

It doesn't require a high-risk portfolio to get these kinds of benefits. In fact, the authors assumed the additional retirement funds would be placed in relatively low-risk investments. As long as the pretax returns on the retirement accounts are greater than the after-tax rates on the mortgage, "households are generally better off saving in a TDA [tax-deferred annuity] instead of prepaying their mortgage."[41]

As in all things, however, I would suggest that a balance is called for. No debt is as bad as too much debt. I used to be a zero-debt advocate, but now I think zero debt can create a diversification and liquidity problem. If I have too much of my net worth tied up in home equity, I am very sensitive to falling real estate prices, and I am going to find it very difficult to tap my equity if I need it.

The problem with home equity is that the more I need it, the harder it is to get to. What lender, for instance, is going to give me a home equity loan when I have just lost my job? What kind of bargaining power do I have in the sale of my home if a loved one is sick and needs hugely expensive out-of-pocket medical treatment?

On the other hand, I am not an advocate of taking the money you would use to pay off a mortgage and investing it in high-risk investments. I would not, for example, recommend you play the arbitrage game between mortgage rates and mutual fund returns, as many salespeople are suggesting these days.

Similarly, I would never recommend taking a loan for the specific purpose of investing that money. I state in my own investment method, however, that I will borrow very small amounts on margin from time to time to take advantage of some extra leverage. So there is definitely a line. Personally, I am still trying to define exactly where I draw that line. It's sort of like what the judge said about pornography: I know it when I see it, but I have a hard time defining it.

chapter 8

TAKE FULL ADVANTAGE OF TAX-DEFERRED RETIREMENT ACCOUNTS

Little by little you can safely stack up a strong reserve here,
but not until after you start.
—Sign in a bank window

TAX-DEFERRED ACCOUNTS, SUCH as a 401(k), a 403(b), SIMPLE plans, and IRAs, have advantages over taxable accounts that can really add up over time. Among these advantages are

1. Return on investment is not immediately taxed, leaving more money in the account to benefit from compounding returns.
2. It is harder for you to rob your tax-deferred accounts. The taxes and ten-percent early withdrawal penalty act as a big deterrent.

3. These accounts are generally protected from creditors if you should ever file for bankruptcy or get sued.

Max out your tax-deferred retirement accounts. If you are covered by a 401(k), 403(b), SIMPLE, or other similar type plan at work, contribute the maximum the law allows each year. If you cannot contribute the maximum, be sure to at least contribute enough to get the entire employer match.

To calculate the amount you must contribute to get the full match from an employer, take the percentage of pay they limit the match to, called the match level, and divide it by the match rate. The answer is how much you have to contribute to take full advantage of the free money your employer is willing to kick in. For example, to get the full match from an employer who matches 50 cents on the dollar up to 6 percent of pay, you would divide .06 by .5. This tells you to contribute 12 percent of pay to get the full company match.

EXCEPTION — VARIABLE ANNUITIES

You will notice that the title of this chapter is "Take full advantage of tax-deferred *retirement* accounts." This does not mean that all tax-deferred accounts are created equal. Some you should stay away from or even avoid like the plague. Variable annuities fall into this category.

A couple of years ago, I was invited to speak at a large investment conference. I mentioned that I am opposed to stock picking, actively managed mutual funds, and variable annuities. An advisor came up to me afterward and questioned me on why I didn't like variable annuities.

My first observation is that everyone who sells annuities seems to be enamored with them. Imagine that! They pay some of the heftiest commissions an advisor can find. My question is, Why are the *only* people enamored with them the people who sell them?

But hang on a minute. I'm getting ahead of myself. Let's go back to some basics.

Harold Evensky says the word *annuity* is like the word *cancer*. It is very broad and widely used, but it can mean so many very different things. So, let's be clear what we're talking about.

We can broadly divide annuities up into a matrix. On one axis is the time period in which the annuity payment begins: immediate or deferred. On the other axis is the variability of the annuity payment: fixed or variable.

The category I have such a problem with is the variable annuity. A single-premium immediate annuity may very well have a place in a retirement portfolio to guarantee a minimum income level, especially for the person who is retiring on a very small amount of money.

But variable annuities are a different deal altogether. The truth is, the percentage of people that a variable or equity indexed annuity is appropriate for is absolutely minuscule. Yet, they are being sold left and right to everybody and his dog! I think that's egregious.

I have written numerous articles and spoken to this topic on my radio show countless times. I've also been interviewed, along with other experts, on the subject. You can find all of them archived on my blog. But to summarize, here are my beefs with variable annuities, whether they be the traditional, the principal protected, or the equity indexed variety.

- Expenses and commissions are too high. This creates a conflict of interest for both the broker who sells them and the insurance company that manages them.
- They are tax disadvantaged in three very meaningful ways, in spite of the fact that they are sold as being tax advantaged.
- The underlying assets are mutual funds, called subaccounts. We know the majority of regular mutual funds under-perform the market in any given year. Studies show variable annuity subac-

counts perform even worse because of the higher fees they have to overcome.

- You can't get your money without penalty for anywhere from seven to ten years.
- The sales practices are abusive. Generally, the only person the variable annuity is appropriate for is someone who is very young, has a long enough time horizon to actually get some benefit from the structure, has a very high income level, and is maxing out all other tax-deferred accounts. Yet, these annuities are being sold day in, day out to the very opposite sort of person; namely, to older people near, or very near, to retirement. That's just wrong.
- Many of these deferred annuities are being put inside IRAs. That's also just wrong. A tax-deferred account inside a tax-deferred account makes no sense except to the person receiving the 6 percent commission.

To summarize, for 99.99 percent of people, I think buying a variable or equity indexed annuity is basically committing "annuicide."

SHOULD I STOP CONTRIBUTING TO MY 401(K) IF I THINK I CAN GET A HIGHER RETURN ELSEWHERE?

This is a tough question for me. Unfortunately, I get it all the time. The problem arises because I can make equally cogent arguments both for and against this practice. In the end, however, I have come down on the side of saying no. Do not stop contributing to your 401(k), even if you think you can do better by directing your own investments.

There is no question that a 401(k), 403(b), or other similar type of plan has shortcomings. The following list shows the main ones:

1. You are generally limited to mutual funds, and then only the mutual funds offered by your particular plan (unless you are lucky enough to work for the small percentage of employers who offer a brokerage window in their plan, which allows you to self-direct all or part of the funds).
2. The smaller your employer, the worse the mutual funds tend to be.
3. The choices for managing risk tend to be very limited. Bond and money market funds tend to get very little attention when these plans are being designed.
4. The fees are hidden. You have no idea if you are paying a lot or a little. In fact, most people don't even know they are paying fees in their 401(k).
5. Even after the Pension Protection Act of 2006, some estate planning headaches continue to go along with these types of plans. IRAs are still better than annuities for estate planning purposes.

But even having said all that, I still think the benefits outweigh the shortcomings. You may think you are going to get a better return, but unless you have a systematic investment strategy, like the Snider Investment Method®,* chances are equally good that you could do worse. (I do not mean to imply that my investment method will always outperform a 401[k]. Empirical evidence does suggest, however, that using a systematic investment methodology can reduce costly investment mistakes that reduce investor returns.)

I also like the fact that you are more likely to save and less likely to rob from your plan if you set it on autopilot and forget it. Finally, there is the issue of protection from creditors, which is not insignificant in this day and age.

So the short answer is if an employer-sponsored plan is available to you, take advantage of it and max it out.

---

*See the appendix for disclosures relating to the Snider Investment Method® and the Snider Investment Method Workshop.

ROLL YOUR 401(K) OVER INTO AN IRA AS SOON AS YOU LEAVE AN EMPLOYER

A few years back my husband and I were on our way to the airport to fly to Phoenix for my grandmother's 85th-birthday celebration. We were listening to an investment show on the radio (not mine, obviously). A caller asked the host whether or not he should roll his 401(k) over into an IRA when he left his old employer. The host emphatically replied yes, the caller should not leave his 401(k) with his former employer.

Then the caller said, "I've always heard that. Can you tell me why that is?" The host then explained that you are in danger of losing your 401(k) if your former employer goes out of business.

The radio show host gave the right answer, but then he gave the wrong reason! Your employer, current or former, is not the custodian of your 401(k) account. The employer doesn't hold the money. A third party does.

The primary reason you want to roll your 401(k) over into an IRA as soon as you leave an employer is that you have more investment alternatives in an IRA than in a 401(k). In a 401(k), you are limited to the mutual funds offered by your plan administrator. In an IRA, you can buy and sell the entire universe of investment alternatives, including all stocks, bonds, mutual funds, options, real estate, and even privately held companies.

While that is the most important reason to roll your 401(k) over into an IRA when you leave, there are others.

- If invested properly, your fees will be lower in an IRA than a 401(k), and as we will learn in the section on investing, lower fees are like risk-free return.
- There is easier access to your money, but I'm not sure this is such a good thing. If you want to rob your retirement account, you needn't ask for permission, nor is there any bureaucratic paperwork.
- You can split IRAs for multiple beneficiaries.

- IRAs are easier to allocate when you have non-spousal heirs.

The steps for rolling over a 401(k) or similar plan to an IRA are very simple.

1. Decide what bank, brokerage firm, insurance company, or mutual fund company you are going to use for your new IRA.
2. Set up an IRA at that institution if you don't have one already.
3. Fill out the paperwork at your old employer requesting a direct transfer of the old plan into your new IRA.
4. Wait. The transfer can take anywhere from a few weeks to a month or more.
5. Confirm. Make sure everything was transferred out of the old plan, that everything made it into the new plan, and that nothing was sent or paid to you in error.

Even though they are simple, let's go through the steps one by one in a bit more detail.

Step number one is to decide where you are going to put your new IRA. You have many choices. You can put your IRA at a bank, a mutual fund company, an insurance company (heaven forbid), or a brokerage firm (either full service or online). Your decision will be based on several factors, such as fees, commissions, the number of investment options, and the customer service provided.

My advice is that you stay away from anyone who charges you fees. You want a firm that has no inactivity fees, no IRA fees, no account closure fees, etc. Many firms advertise cheap commissions and then they kill you with fees. But there are plenty more with no fees at all. What you see is what you get.

Speaking of commissions, you want those to be minimal. Commissions are especially meaningful in a small account and, while you have to balance commissions with other factors, you want commissions to be reasonable.

Investment options are also an important factor. You don't want to be limited in your investment options. One of the old saws in investing says, "Never mix insurance and investing." You don't want to be limited to just mutual funds or annuities. One of the big benefits of moving to an IRA is the wide range of investment alternatives, so make sure all are available wherever you choose.

Finally, you have to determine how much service and advice you want or will need. I hope you would check either the box marked "little" or "none" because you are educating yourself and you're able to do it yourself. Realistically, of course, not everyone is going to do that. Realizing what level of service you will need will help you determine where you put your IRA.

Step number two (once you have selected where your account is going) is to set up the account. With most brokerage firms, this is quite easy. You fill out an account application, either online or at their office. You don't have to put any money in the account at this stage; this paperwork just opens the account.

In years past, tax law differentiated between rollover IRAs and traditional IRAs. Unless you plan to someday roll the money back into a company plan (which I don't recommend—that is why you got it out in the first place), you can just roll your 401(k) over into a traditional IRA. There is no longer a need to set it up as a rollover IRA, and your 401(k) funds can be mixed with a traditional IRA if you already have one.

Step number three (once the account is set up and you receive an account number) is to fill out the paperwork requesting a direct transfer.

This step is very important. You generally get the paperwork from the HR department at your old employer or the administrator of your old plan. When you fill out this paperwork, you want to specify that the funds from your old plan be sent directly to the custodian of your new IRA.

The reason for this is that you have 60 days in which to deposit any retirement plan distributions into your IRA or you will owe taxes and penalties. When you move the money between custodians directly, there can be no chance of a costly misstep on your part. You just give them the name of the new IRA custodian and your account number and let them transfer the money.

If your old plan administrator refuses to do a direct transfer (very few still won't), then you want to make sure they make the check out in the name of the new custodian, with your account number on it, rather than to you directly. You also want to ensure that they do not withhold taxes so that you are not forced to make up the shortfall when depositing it into the new account. Lastly, make sure you deposit the funds right away. As I said earlier, though, almost every plan will transfer directly to your IRA nowadays.

Step number four is easy. You wait. It may take anywhere from a few weeks to a month or more for a transfer of this type to take place. Even though it has gotten much faster over the years, many employees still complain about how long it takes to move funds out of their old plan.

Step number five, the last step, is to confirm, confirm, confirm. Don't assume. There may be some difference between the balance on the last statement from your old plan and the balance by the time it gets to your IRA because the value of the securities in the account will have changed. But, you must make certain that all of the money was transferred out of the old account and all of it arrived safely in the new IRA. The IRS doesn't accept "I forgot" or "I didn't check" as an excuse when they are assessing penalties and taxes.

Provided you follow these five steps, you will probably find that the rollover process wasn't nearly as hard as you thought it was going to be.

And, for those of you who know you should roll that money out of an old plan but were afraid because you didn't know how to do it, now you know. Trust me, it is much simpler than buying a car, so don't procrastinate any longer. Get that old 401(k) into where it belongs.

LOANS FROM YOUR RETIREMENT PLAN

Simply put, we raid our plans in three different ways: (1) hardship withdrawals; (2) loans; and (3) cashing out when we leave our employer instead of rolling the money over into an IRA. If I wanted to, I could make this section very short. The rule is: Never ever raid your plan—for any reason.

Retirement funds should be sacrosanct, untouchable. One tip I always tell people to use to reinforce this idea is this: When you get in a bind and start thinking about raiding your retirement funds, get creative and imagine what you would do if you didn't have any money saved for retirement. Would you borrow money from family, take a second job, pick up cans on the side of the road? Whatever it is you would do, do that! Don't take the easy way out.

The temptation is to sacrifice the future because you have a need or a desire today. We are eternal optimists. We always tell ourselves we will make it up later, but we never do. The fact is that you have far more options when you are young than when you are old. Resist the temptation to rob from the old lady or old man you will someday become and figure out some other way.

See? I told you I could make this section short. I'll very quickly go through hardship withdrawals, loans, and cashing out so you are familiar with them, but if you bought this book because you have financial success as an objective, don't do any of the things I am about to tell you about. OK?

Let's start with hardship withdrawals. A hardship withdrawal isn't a loan. The IRS makes it difficult to take a hardship withdrawal and imposes stiff penalties when you take one. The IRS allows hardship withdrawals only under the following conditions:

> (1) the withdrawal is due to an immediate and heavy financial need; (2) the withdrawal must be necessary to satisfy that need [i.e., you have no other funds or way to meet the need]; (3) the withdrawal must not exceed the amount needed by you; (4) you must have first obtained all distribution or nontaxable loans available under the 401(k) plan; and (5) you can't contribute to the 401(k) plan for six months following the withdrawal.[42]

Financial hardship withdrawals are allowed for the following circumstances:

- To buy a primary residence
- To prevent foreclosure or eviction from your home
- To pay college tuition due within the next 12 months for yourself or a dependent
- To pay un-reimbursed medical expenses
- To pay funeral expenses
- For the repair of your primary residence[43]

You will always owe taxes on a withdrawal from a traditional 401(k), 403(b), or SIMPLE plan. If you are under 59½ years old, you will also pay a 10 percent early withdrawal penalty unless you:

- Become totally disabled
- Have medical expenses that exceed 7.5 percent of your adjusted gross income
- Have died and your beneficiaries get the money

- Are required by a court to give the money to a divorced spouse, child, or dependent
- Are permanently laid off, terminated, quit, or retired in the same year you turn 55 or later
- You are permanently laid off, terminated, quit, or retired and have established a schedule of regular withdrawals in equal amounts based on your expected lifespan.[44]

The withdrawals referred to in the last item are also called 72(t) withdrawals or substantially equal payments and the withdrawals must continue for five years or until you reach age 59½, whichever is longer.

When you are desperate for money, a hardship withdrawal may look like the easy answer. What many people don't realize, though, is that a $10,000 withdrawal doesn't equal $10,000 in your pocket. If you are under 59½ years of age, you'll lose between 35 percent and 45 percent—or $3,500 to $4,500—to taxes and penalties!

Not only that, but what seems like a little now is really a lot later on. Imagine that you contribute $5,000 a year to your retirement plan beginning at age 30 and get an average return of 8 percent. At age 40, you take $10,000 out of your plan for the down payment on a house. At age 65, you will have $793,094. But if you hadn't taken the $10,000, you would have $861,584, or $68,490 more. All of us promise ourselves that we'll put back the money we borrow, but few of us ever do.

Employers are not required to offer hardship withdrawals. Some do and some don't. Your employer may offer them for some circumstances, but not for others. If your plan does offer them, they will be spelled out in the summary plan description available from your HR department.

The same is true of loans from your plan. About 20 percent of plans offer a loan provision. Typically, you will be allowed to borrow up to 50 percent of the amount in your plan, up to a limit of $50,000. In almost all cases, you have to repay the loan in 60 equal monthly payments over a five-year term. The interest rate is determined on the day you take the loan and is often the prime rate plus 1 percent. Almost all companies will deduct your loan payments from your paycheck, and you can repay the full amount of the loan at any time without penalties.[45]

While loans may be convenient, they are rarely the right answer. There is a popular misconception that paying back a 401(k) loan is like paying yourself. That is not true. When you take a loan from your plan, you are taking money out. It no longer has the ability to earn a return. The interest you pay is not a return because it comes from you instead of someone else. It is just moving your money from one place to another.

There are two disadvantages to 401(k) loans: (1) while the loan is outstanding, you are losing the benefits of tax-deferred profits; and (2) if you leave your employer for any reason—you are terminated, are laid off, or quit—the entire amount is due immediately. If you can't repay it, you are placed in default. The IRS will treat the defaulted amount as a distribution.

If you are under 59½ years of age, you will not only owe both state and federal taxes but also the 10 percent penalty. Depending on what state you live in, that could amount to 50 percent of the loan balance payable to Uncle Sam.

Of course, no one thinks they are going to lose their job when they take the loan. But it happens. If you could afford to repay the loan in one pop, you wouldn't need the loan in the first place! In fact, just a short time ago I received an e-mail from a woman who was in this very situation. She had borrowed from her 401(k) and then lost her job. Now she owes the IRS $18,000 in taxes and she doesn't have it. She was writing to me for suggestions. Unfortunately, in a situation like this, there are very few options.

And one final note on 401(k) loans. I never, ever recommend you borrow from your 401(k) to invest. Sometimes people are tempted by the promise of higher returns outside their retirement plan than they can get inside the plan plus the interest. That is never a guarantee. Remember, pigs get fat, but hogs get slaughtered. Don't be greedy or dumb with your retirement funds.

Speaking of dumb, don't cash out your plan when you leave your employer. You always want to roll the money over into an IRA as outlined above, even if the amount is small. Don't fall into the trap of saying, "Oh, but it's just one/three/five thousand dollars." Roll it over into an IRA.

There are two exceptions to the rule. One is when you have highly appreciated company stock. The other is when you have after-tax money in your 401(k). The latter is a pretty rare occurrence, but if you find yourself in this situation, you might find it easier to just roll the after-tax portion over into a taxable account rather than to continue to do the paperwork to calculate your basis. You should consult with a qualified tax professional in both of these cases to determine the best course of action.

chapter 9

SAVE FOR RETIREMENT FIRST, THEN YOUR KIDS' COLLEGE

*There is a certain Buddhistic calm that comes
from having . . . money in the bank.*
—Tim Robbins

PARENTS TODAY ARE CAUGHT between the proverbial rock and a hard place. You will need at least a million dollars put away to support a fairly modest retirement, a good deal more if your lifestyle requirements are more upscale. And then there is college for the kiddos. College tuition at an exclusive private school can run as much as $50,000 a year. For example, tuition at Southern Methodist University, here in Dallas where I live, is $30,880 a year plus $10,000 a year for room and board.[46] Out-of-state tuition at a public school, like the University of Colorado–Boulder where I went to school, is $22,989 for 2008. For in-state residents it is just $5,643, plus $8,300 for room and board.[47]

So the questions are: Which comes first? How can we do both? Should we do both?

If we start comparing ourselves to parents with grown children, it is easy to get an inferiority complex. They somehow managed to do both. How come I am finding it so hard? If it makes you feel any better, they had some advantages you don't.

The post–World War II years saw an unprecedented explosion in families' purchasing power. Many employers offered pension plans to employees, so saving for retirement wasn't a requirement for many. For those that had them, either from their employer or their military service, pensions offered a guaranteed income for life.

My parents had me when my mother was 18 and my father was 20. My father's parents married when they were 16. Parents started families earlier, giving them more time to save. Early retirement wasn't even in the vocabulary. My great-grandfather was still working on the farm well into his 90s. Ask today's workers the ideal age to retire and the average answer is 55.[48] So, comparisons might not be valid. You live in a different time with different variables.

An annual survey sponsored by Allstate revealed that 46 percent of respondents split their savings equally between retirement and college savings. If this were a question on a college exam, the 14 percent who were saving for college[49] would have flunked! The answer in today's world is mathematically simple, even if it sounds somewhat coldhearted. Saving for retirement has to come first.

Let's use an example to show why. Imagine a couple, Bob and Sue. Their total household income is $100,000. They invest 6 percent of their income every year for 36 years. Assume they get an 8 percent return and every year their pay increases by 3 percent.

If, for the first 18 years, Bob and Sue divide their savings between retirement and college and then, for the last 18 years, they switch their focus solely to retirement, they would have $126,000 in college savings and $1.65 million in retirement savings.

Now imagine, instead, that Bob and Sue save only for college the first 18 years and only for retirement the last 18 years. They would have $253,000 in college savings and just $759,000 in retirement savings. And that assumes they get a 50 percent match from their employer in their retirement account.

Remember this truism: Your kids can borrow to go to college, but no one will lend you money for your retirement. Because so many of us had our college paid for, we feel an obligation to do the same for our kids. We don't want them to think, "Mom and Dad had all that money socked away and saddled me with all these student loans." Trust me. Having to take care of you financially in your old age will be a much bigger burden on them than student loans will be.

(Allow me this observation from my own experience. My father paid for my college education; my husband paid his own way through both undergraduate and graduate school with scholarships and part-time work. I have to admit I think Jim valued his education more as a result of having to work for it. I don't think I would have taken college nearly so lightly if I had to work for it.)

Another good reason to save for retirement first is that the formula for financial aid doesn't include money in retirement accounts when it calculates how much your family can afford. Money in your retirement accounts reduces the amount available for college expenses and therefore increases your son's or daughter's chances of receiving financial aid.

Bottom line: Make sure you have your retirement squared away before you start putting money away for your child's/children's college. If you are still determined to put your offspring's education first, however, just make sure you fully understand the consequences. The decision you are making could mean working for the rest of your life or depending on the kindness of strangers in your old age.

Your kids are going to hold many things against you by the time they become adults. I know I sure did. This is just one of many. Believe me, they'll get over it as they get older.

SECTION FOUR

Invest Wisely

chapter 10

DETERMINE YOUR MONEY'S HIGHER PURPOSE

To accomplish great things, we must dream as well as act.
—J. A. F. Thibault

MIKE CALLED INTO MY radio show one Saturday afternoon. He had gotten very aggressive in his allocations in his 401(k). At that point in time, since the market had been going up for a while, he was nervous and wanted to know whether or not he should change his allocations to something more conservative.

Mike was contemplating changing his portfolio based on what he thought the market might do in the future. This is called market timing, and it is doomed to failure. Stock picking and market timing are by-products of an obsession with day-to-day performance, which is a surefire way to get the opposite result.

In my experience I've worked with thousands of individual investors. What I've found is that most of us put the cart before the horse.

Like Mike, we work from the bottom up instead of the top down. We decide how much to save, what vehicles to save our money in, what insurance products to buy, and even what investment strategies to follow without having a vision that drives those decisions.

Vision without action is a daydream.
Action without vision is a nightmare.

—Japanese proverb

Are your finances a nightmare? Start with a vision for You, Inc. What is your money's higher purpose? What are your objectives? Why are you putting your money to work? What do you want it to help you achieve?

Please be aware that this issue is not about numbers. Your objective isn't an 8 percent return or a million dollars in the bank. Your objective is all about what you are able to do with your financial success. This is about being able to do what you want, when you want, without worrying how you are going to pay for it. And most likely, your objective isn't going to be just one thing. It may be several.

I have one client who, in his mid-50s—his peak earning years—took two years off to do missionary work in Africa. I have another client who left his job to take care of his two sons full time. Now he is getting his teaching certificate so he can be on the same schedule as his boys as they grow older.

Maybe your vision is a little bit more mundane. You just want to have enough money to be able to quit working sometime before you die. That's OK. But I would encourage you to allow yourself to get creative and think big.

What really lights your fire? What is the one thing you secretly want to do if you had enough money and enough courage? That one thing is your money's higher purpose.

In the long run, you only hit what you aim at.
—Henry David Thoreau

The cool thing about approaching money this way—even if you don't hit what you aim at—is that if you aim high enough, even a miss will put you in a pretty good position. So why not aim high?

Once you understand your money's higher purpose, you have three other factors to consider before you can even begin to think about which investments to put your money to work in. Those three factors are (1) consider where you fall on the risk-reward continuum; (2) consider your temperament; and (3) consider your time horizon.

Investments stretch along a risk-reward continuum. At one end of that continuum are investments that produce a guaranteed return; at the other end are investments that offer the chance, but not the promise, of a return. Generally speaking, the higher the return the higher the risk. It should be noted, though, that risk can take many different forms; it is not always simply the loss of capital. You need to think about where you fall on this risk-reward continuum. That's where your temperament comes in.

What sort of investor are you? Are you patient or impatient? Do you stick with an idea that makes sense, or do you change philosophy every time what you are doing begins to feel the slightest bit uncomfortable? How hands-on are you? How much time do you want to spend managing your investments? These are all questions pertaining to temperament.

Finally, there is a time horizon. We all have to stop thinking of our investment time horizon as our retirement date. Our investment time horizon is as long as we will live. That is how long our money has to work for us. Not just until the day we retire. For almost everyone reading this, we are talking a minimum of 20 years; for most of you, much longer.

Aim at heaven and you will get earth thrown in.
Aim at earth and you get neither.

—C. S. Lewis

I am 44. For planning purposes, I assume my investment time horizon will stretch to the age of 102. In other words, my investment time horizon is 58 years! With that sort of time horizon, if I plan to hold an equity-based portfolio for that long, what risk do I have? Not much.

Will I experience temporary declines in my portfolio value? Of course. Markets are cyclical; they go up and down. But at the end of 58 years, how likely is it that my investment will not have grown at a rate that exceeds the total return on bonds? As my grandmother used to say, "Nothing's impossible, just highly improbable." Get it?

Assuming a time horizon that is too short causes you to see monsters under the bed that really don't exist. We'll talk more about managing risk in future chapters. For now, be aware that it is your life expectancy, not your retirement date, which determines your investment time horizon.

Only when you are crystal clear on these four things—your money's higher purpose, where you fall on the risk-reward continuum, your temperament, and your time horizon—can you begin to choose the investment philosophy that is best suited to your specific needs. Yet, when

I ask a room full of investors how many of them can tell me what their money's higher purpose is, only one in ten typically raises their hand.

When you get clear about these things before choosing an investment, questions like Mike's go away. Investment strategies and specific investment vehicles are chosen based on their ability to achieve your objectives with the appropriate amount of risk, and no more, and their ability to fit your temperament and time horizon.

When you take this top-down approach, your investments—in other words, your money's place of employment—should change only when one of these four things changes. And that, I shouldn't need to tell you, should occur very infrequently. A change in economic or market conditions does not constitute a reason to change your portfolio.

Courage is never to let your actions
be influenced by your fears.

—Arthur Koestler

An investor who takes this approach is a courageous investor. A courageous investor never changes course based on fits of fear or greed. The beauty is that the level of commitment to the investment approach matches the level of commitment to the objective. Provided you are committed to your money's highest purpose, the rest becomes a moot point.

chapter 11

KNOW YOUR STRENGTHS AND WEAKNESSES

We must not be hampered by yesterday's myths
in concentrating on today's needs.
—Harold S. Geneen

A FUNDAMENTAL ECONOMIC PRINCIPLE is that investors are perfectly logical. Economic theory assumes we process all known information, learn from our mistakes, and then make the decision that will maximize "utility." Of course, that is a bunch of hooey. We are not robots, and we don't react logically. Anyone who has ever invested in the stock market knows that.

How we really act, and why, is the realm of behavioral finance. Here is an excerpt from an article in *The Australian*, to validate the point.

Late at night, in a basement laboratory at Stanford University, Brian Knutson made a startling discovery: our brains lust after money, just like they crave sex.

It was May 2004, and Knutson, a professor of neuroscience and psychology at the California university, was sending student volunteers through a high-power imaging machine called an MRI.

Deep inside each subject's head, electrical currents danced through a bundle of neurons about the size and shape of a peanut. Blood was rushing to the brain's pleasure centre as students executed mock stock and bond trades. On Knutson's screen, this region of the brain, the core of human desire, flashed canary yellow.

The pleasure of orgasm, the high from cocaine, the rush of buying Google at $US450 a share—the same neural network governs all three, Knutson, 38, concluded. What's more, our primal pleasure circuits can, and often do, override our seat of reason, the brain's frontal cortex, the professor says. In other words, stocks, like sex, sometimes drive us crazy.[50]

The stock market is people.

—Bernard Baruch

Key to investing wisely is recognizing that emotions are our worst enemy. Emotions cause us to do the opposite of what we should be doing. Emotions cause us to buy when we should be selling and to sell when we should be buying.

So, in order to be a successful investor, you must learn how to (1) ignore your emotional response; (2) train yourself to act opposite to what your emotions would tell you to do; and (3) most importantly, adopt a rigid system that keeps you from responding emotionally.

I have often said this is the real value in the Snider Investment Method®. While it is most certainly an innovative way to create high yield with a reasonable risk trade-off,* it is, at its core, a behavior modification system as much as it is a system for creating cash flow from your portfolio.

This is critically important. The performance of the investment does not matter. It is the investor's behavior that will ultimately determine the investor's return.

Consider a classic experiment conducted in 1948 by B. F. Skinner. Paul Slovic describes the experiment as follows:

> Skinner found that hungry birds, given food at brief random intervals, developed very idiosyncratic, repetitive actions. The precise form of this behavior varied from bird to bird, and Skinner referred to these actions as superstitions. What happened to these birds can be described in terms of the concept of positive reinforcement. The delivery of food increased the likelihood of whatever form of behavior happened to precede it. Food was then presented again. Because the reinforced behavior was occurring at an increased rate, it was more likely to be reinforced again. The second reinforcement caused a further increase in the rate of this particular behavior which improved its chances of being reinforced again, and so on. After a short while the birds were found to be turning rapidly counter clockwise about the cage, hopping from side to side, making odd head

---

*See the appendix for disclosures relating to the Snider Investment Method® and the Snider Investment Method Workshop.

movements, etc. Because such behaviors are reinforced less than 100 percent of the time during learning, they persist even when reinforcement stops altogether. Animals trained in this way have been known to make many as 10,000 attempts to obtain a reward that was no longer forthcoming.[51]

You don't need to be very creative to see the similarities between investing in the stock market and Skinner's classic experiment with birds, do you? Both produce massive amounts of data—perfect to draw illusory correlations from. The expected outcome, an increase in wealth, would certainly be a positive. That increase in wealth is associated with a positive reinforcement, good performance, which is certainly inter- mittent if not random. And finally, there is little feedback to refute the illusory correlation. Few people take the time to do the statistically valid studies required to prove to themselves that a chart pattern, for example, is nothing more than what Skinner called a superstition!

I see this time and time again among investors. Imagine that I buy ten different stocks, and all the stocks whose company names begin with the letter "A" go up in price while the others all go down. The heuristics, or logical shortcuts in our brain's operating system, cause us to leap to an illusory correlation between the company name and rising stock prices. Consequently, I start buying more stocks in companies whose names begin with A. A random distribution of returns in a ris- ing market would suggest, incorrectly, that stocks beginning with A go up more often than not. With an ever-increasing percentage of stocks in my portfolio beginning with A, I cannot see that stocks that begin with other letters go up in equal percentages.

You may say, "That's ridiculous!" Admittedly, I made the example extreme to illustrate the idea. But make it somewhat plausible, and people do it all the time without realizing.

Let's take the investment technique known as technical analysis as an example. If I buy several stocks when they rise above their 20-day moving average and I make money on them, I will create an illusory correlation between the two. As long as I can spot the pattern sometimes and make money on it, which reinforces the correlation in my mind, I will continue to look for it and bet on it. It doesn't matter that the pattern often fails to hold true. I will continue to believe in the correlation.

To make the correlation in our minds is very easy. It requires merely a tenuous association between an event and a reward. But to disprove the correlation is quite hard. Few people are going to sit down and calculate the correlation coefficient between price and the 20-day moving average.

Having a quote machine on your desk is like having a slot machine there.

—Ed Seykota

I also find the link between these behaviors and addictions to be striking. What makes something really addictive is when we receive intermittent variable reinforcement.

"The interesting thing that Skinner discovered about intermittent reinforcement and maybe one of Skinner's most important discoveries was that behavior that is reinforced intermittently is much more difficult to extinguish than behavior that is reinforced continuously."[52]

A slot machine is a perfect example. We put money in and occasionally money comes out—not always, and the amount varies. This is intermittent variable reinforcement. It is this characteristic that makes something really addictive.

E-mail is another example. Do you know anyone who constantly checks e-mail? Why do they do it? Intermittent variable reinforcement. You are not sure what you will get each time, or if you will get anything at all, so you keep checking.

Of course, the leap from gambling to investing is not a big one. Like gamblers, investors get random, or intermittent, reinforcement (profits) that varies in size and frequency. Do you think it is a coincidence that most investors don't buy bonds (which are neither variable nor intermittent) even though portfolio theory says you should have a substantial percentage of bonds in your portfolio? I think one of the most beneficial things an investor can do is to study these sorts of behavioral issues. In fact, I think your time is far better spent in studying behavioral finance than in studying stock charts and trading strategies. Only when we understand that our behavior is far more complex than we probably realize can we hope to overcome our shortcomings as investors. For many of us, our lack of knowledge of investing isn't what screws us up; it's our lack of knowledge about how our own brain functions during the investment process.

chapter 12

START EARLY — SLOW AND STEADY WINS THE RACE

*Here's something to think about: How come you
never see a headline like "Psychic Wins Lottery"?*
—Jay Leno

FINANCIAL SUCCESS IS A product of time, savings, and after-tax return.

FINANCIAL SUCCESS = TIME × SAVINGS × AFTER-TAX RETURN

The variables within the formula are listed according to priority. In other words, time is more powerful than the amount you save. The amount you save is more powerful than the return you get. Where do we tend to put the most focus? You guessed it—return. People have a tendency to work these variables in reverse order.

Time

Let's look at the story of two high school classmates, Burt and Henry. Burt is a talented graphic artist who gets a great job right out of high school that pays $45,000 a year. He is 19 years old, still lives at home with his parents, works day and night, and isn't very social, so his expenses are minimal.

Henry goes to college and then on to graduate school. By the time he gets out of school and starts making any money, he is 27.

Both young men invest $2,000 a year and earn 10 percent. Burt starts at 19, invests for 8 years, and then stops at age 27. Henry can't even start investing until he is 27, and he continues to invest until age 65. Who has more money at age 65, Burt or Henry?

I used this example in a speech I gave to an association a while back. Every single person in the room said Henry. Is that what you said?

The answer is Burt! Burt has $1,035,159 at age 65, and Henry has just $883,185. Even though Burt saved just $16,000 and Henry saved $78,000, Burt's 8-year head start won the day.

More importantly, Henry could never catch up to Burt so long as he continued contributing only $2,000 a year. At age 90, Burt's account would have grown to $11,215,647 and Henry's to only $9,785,414!

This is an example of compounding (see Figure 12.1). Some people say Albert Einstein called compounding the ninth wonder of the world. Turns out he never said it, but compounding is nonetheless a wonder when it comes to building wealth and creating financial success.

Compounding, simply stated, is the exponential effect created when you earn profits on your profits. The more time you give compounding to work, the higher up on that exponential curve you get. In other words, the longer you let your money work for you, the harder it works for you.

FIGURE 12.1

	HENRY AND BURT (ASSUMES A 10% ANNUAL RETURN EACH YEAR FOR BOTH)			
	HENRY		BURT	
Age	Invests	Balance	Invests	Balance
19	$2,000	$2,200	$0	$0
20	$2,000	$4,620	$0	$0
21	$2,000	$7,282	$0	$0
22	$2,000	$10,210	$0	$0
23	$2,000	$13,431	$0	$0
24	$2,000	$16,974	$0	$0
25	$2,000	$20,872	$0	$0
26	$2,000	$25,159	$0	$0
27	$0	$27,675	$2,000	$2,200
28	$0	$30,442	$2,000	$4,620
29	$0	$33,487	$2,000	$7,282
30	$0	$36,835	$2,000	$10,210
31	$0	$40,519	$2,000	$13,431
32	$0	$44,571	$2,000	$16,974
33	$0	$49,028	$2,000	$20,872
34	$0	$53,930	$2,000	$25,159
35	$0	$59,323	$2,000	$29,875
36	$0	$65,256	$2,000	$35,062
37	$0	$71,781	$2,000	$40,769
38	$0	$78,960	$2,000	$47,045
39	$0	$86,856	$2,000	$53,950
40	$0	$95,541	$2,000	$61,545
41	$0	$105,095	$2,000	$69,899
42	$0	$115,605	$2,000	$79,089
43	$0	$127,165	$2,000	$89,198
44	$0	$139,882	$2,000	$100,318
45	$0	$153,870	$2,000	$112,550

continued on page 109

continued from page 108

HENRY AND BURT (ASSUMES A 10% ANNUAL RETURN EACH YEAR FOR BOTH)				
	HENRY		BURT	
Age	Invests	Balance	Invests	Balance
46	$0	$169,257	$2,000	$126,005
47	$0	$186,183	$2,000	$140,805
48	$0	$204,801	$2,000	$157,086
49	$0	$225,281	$2,000	$174,995
50	$0	$247,809	$2,000	$194,694
51	$0	$272,590	$2,000	$216,364
52	$0	$299,849	$2,000	$240,200
53	$0	$329,834	$2,000	$266,420
54	$0	$362,817	$2,000	$295,262
55	$0	$399,099	$2,000	$326,988
56	$0	$439,009	$2,000	$361,887
57	$0	$482,910	$2,000	$400,276
58	$0	$531,201	$2,000	$442,503
59	$0	$584,321	$2,000	$488,953
60	$0	$642,753	$2,000	$540,049
61	$0	$707,028	$2,000	$596,254
62	$0	$777,731	$2,000	$658,079
63	$0	$855,504	$2,000	$726,087
64	$0	$941,054	$2,000	$800,896
65	$0	$1,035,160	$2,000	$883,185

The best time to plant a tree was 20 years ago.
The second best time is now.

—Chinese proverb

The implications of compounding are clear. Start as early as you can and don't put off saving and investing because you don't think you can save enough. Because of compounding, every dollar matters.

Speaking of dollars, here is another compounding brainteaser for you. Imagine you have a single dollar. How many times does it have to double to become a million dollars? A dollar doubled once is two dollars. Double that again, you have four dollars. What's your guess?

The answer is: 20 doubles. How many of you broke out your calculator to get the answer? One dollar doubled 20 times will be $1 million. How close were you? Was your answer much higher? That is because you underestimate the power of compounding.

OK. Now look at some surface, like a table or a desk. Imagine I start at the left-hand edge with a single dollar, and I am trying to get to the right-hand edge, which represents a million dollars. Put your finger on the left edge of the table. After the first double, how much has your finger moved? If the right edge is $1 million, your finger has barely moved, right? That's because the first double gets you only from one dollar to two. And even after several doubles, the movement is almost imperceptible.

Now remember, I said it takes 20 doubles to turn a dollar into a million. After ten doubles, how far down the table do you think your finger would be? After ten doubles, half the number required, you would still have just $1,024!

After the 19th double, where would your finger be? Halfway down the table. The first double got you $1. The last double will get you $500,000! Again, that is an illustration of compounding.

Now let's work this backwards. There's something in investing called the Rule of 72. The Rule of 72 is a quick and dirty rule of thumb that tells you how many years it will take your money to double assuming a given rate of return. The number 72 divided by the rate of return equals approximate years to double.

72 ÷ RETURN % = YEARS TO DOUBLE

The Rule of 72 tells me that if I can average 7.2 percent a year, my portfolio will double every ten years. If I want to retire at age 65 with $1 million, how much do I need at age 55? $500,000. At age 45? $250,000. How about age 35? Just $125,000—an amount that sounds a lot more doable than $1 million, doesn't it?

But here is what happens. You start saving at the left edge of the table. You slog your guts out every day, max out your 401(k), put a little money away, and when your statement comes, it doesn't seem like very much. Ten years into your career, it still isn't very much because you are only at that first double.

At some point, you need a new car or want to buy a bigger house. You look at your retirement savings. It's just sitting there, and it looks so tempting. You think to yourself, I'm probably not going to have enough anyway, so what would borrowing $20,000 hurt? And that is when you hear a flushing sound as any hope of financial success goes right down the drain.

Savings

You can see why time is the most important ally we have when trying to achieve financial success. That is why time comes first in the equation. As the time available decreases, the other two components, savings and return, must increase to make up the difference. Of the two, it is more desirable to increase your savings than to try to increase your return.

Savings is totally within your control. You and you alone decide how much to save. Return percentage is not within your control at all.

Return

In my experience, people who try to increase their return percentage almost always get the opposite result. To increase returns, people become traders rather than investors.

TRADING IS HUNTING.
INVESTING IS FARMING.

Traders are people who change investment strategies or buy and sell investments based on what has happened in the past, what is happening right now, or what they think will happen in the future. Investors are people who choose their investments and strategy based on their objectives and change those investments or strategy only when their objectives change. Many people call themselves investors, but few really are. Most people are really traders.

Dalbar, Inc., a research group out of Boston, produces an annual report called the "Quantitative Analysis of Investor Behavior" (QAIB), which measures "the effects of investor decisions to buy, sell and switch into and out of mutual funds."[53] Year after year, the QAIB shows that "investors"—who are investors in name only; they are really traders—only capture a small fraction of the market returns.

Investment performance doesn't determine real-life returns; investor behavior does.

—Nick Murray

In the 2007 QAIB, Dalbar charts the growth of a $10,000 stock mutual fund investment over 20 years mimicking the trading pattern of the average investor. Then it charts the growth mimicking a systematic investor who, year in and year out, invests the same amount and follows the same strategy regardless of what the market or the individual components of the portfolio are doing. The hunter, or average investor, has $23,252 at the end of 20 years. The farmer, or systematic investor, has $32,877.[54]

Commenting on those findings, Dalbar's staff wrote, "The 40% advantage of systematic investing shows the importance of consistency in wealth building."[55]

Before we see how this works in real life, let me first provide you with a little background. Stock prices are random. This is not a theory; it's a mathematical fact. In 1900, a French mathematician by the name of Louis Bachelier first proposed the idea that stock prices are random.

Since that time, economists and mathematicians have not spent their time debating the truth of that statement so much as debating what mathematical model to use to describe the random movement of prices. Should the model be a Gaussian curve (better known as a bell curve), a Levy progression, or a Brownian motion? The question is not: Are stock prices random? The question is: How do we describe the randomness?

This is a very difficult thing for us mere mortals to get our brains around. Why? First, because we are constantly bombarded by messages that say we can predict the future direction of stocks. Otherwise, how would anyone sell you anything? I can hear the talking heads on FOX or CNN now:

> "The market went down 311 points today. It was the second biggest drop in 2007," says trader Fred from the floor of the New York Stock Exchange.
> The talking head responds, "Fred, what do traders think caused the drop?"

"Oh, we don't know. Nobody knows."

"Well, what do you think will happen tomorrow? Do you think we'll see more profit taking?"

"Don't know. Tomorrow could be up. It could be down."

That would sell a lot of advertising, wouldn't it?

The bigger reason why we find randomness so difficult to grasp is that our brains are not wired to accept this truth. Psychologically, we are optimistic by nature. We all want to believe we will be the one that chance favors. We buy lottery tickets and play the slot machines, certain we will be the one to win, even though the odds say otherwise.

Physiologically, our brains have been hardwired, over millions of years, to see patterns after three occurrences. That's what got us to the top of the food chain. "I have eaten this root three times and I didn't die; therefore, this must be an edible root." That ability to see patterns is one of our survival skills. The challenge that ability presents us with, on the other hand, is that we will see patterns where they don't exist. Sports statistics are the classic example. Stock prices are another.

When we accept that stock prices are random, what we are saying is that no one can accurately predict the future direction of price accurately over long periods of time beyond what we would expect given the laws of chance. Basically, it's a coin flip. Heads, a stock's price goes up. Tails, it goes down.

If stock prices are random, then by extension so is the performance of any given stock mutual fund. Heads, the fund performs better than the market. Tails, it performs worse than the market.

Past performance is no guarantee of future results.
—Standard disclaimer

I'm betting most of you reading this book either own a stock mutual fund today or have owned one sometime in the past. Let's use your 401(k) for our example since your choices in a 401(k) are generally limited to mutual funds. How did you choose which mutual funds to put your money in from within the choices in your 401(k)?

I ask this question of the audience in many of the speeches I give. Almost immediately someone will shout out "past performance," and everyone's head will nod. Most people will choose the fund or funds that have done best over the last five years or so. So, in essence, what we have just done is picked the fund whose fund manager just flipped heads five times in a row.

Because our brain is wired to see patterns and to believe they will continue, this fund is a logical choice because we believe the chances are good that the fund manager will continue to flip heads. But in reality, the chances are still 50/50. Pretty soon, what do you think will happen?

You guessed it. The fund manager flips tails and the fund under-performs. This doesn't feel good, especially if you are focused on short-term performance. If your thinking is, "I need to get as much return as possible," an under-performing fund isn't going to have any place in your portfolio. So you sell it. What have you done? Right! You have just bought it high and sold it low.

Now that you have sold the fund, you have to replace it with something. How do you pick? Right again! The same way! You go back to the list and find the fund with the best five-year return. Once again, you've just picked the fund manager who flipped heads five times in a row. What comes next? Tails! So you sell. And the cycle repeats itself over and over again.

This hunting mentality, or obsession with short-term return, leads to a pattern of buying high and selling low instead of what we are trying to do, which is buy low and sell high. This is what I call the

"Performance Paradox." This behavior is what accounts for the massive differential between investment return and investor return, as measured by Dalbar. In the 20 years ending 2006, the average equity mutual *fund* returned 10.6 percent,[56] while the average equity mutual fund *investor* earned less than half of that, or 4.3 percent.[57]

Of the three variables in the financial success equation—time, savings, and after-tax returns—time is the best. How much you save is the most controllable variable. Trying to increase returns is the variable most likely to backfire.

chapter 13

INVEST YOUR OWN MONEY

A stockbroker is someone who invests
other people's money until it is all gone.
—Woody Allen

INVESTMENT MANAGERS

ACCORDING TO A RECENT groundbreaking study, the raw returns of equally weighted mutual funds (net of all expenses) for 1996 to 2002 were 6.626 percent for investors working on their own and 2.924 percent for funds chosen by advisors.[58]

In other words, the do-it-yourselfer did more than 100 percent better than financial advisors when it came to selecting equity mutual funds. After factoring in inflation and taxes, clients of financial advisors lost money and lost purchasing power. This should be criminal.

The study, "Assessing the Costs and Benefits of Brokers in the Mutual Fund Industry," was written by Daniel Bergstresser and Peter Tufano of Harvard Business School and John Chalmers of the University of Oregon. You are going to be hearing a lot more about this study in the months and years to come. Some are calling it one of the seminal studies of the decade, like those done on asset allocation in the past.

The three professors have written an exhaustive analysis of the cost and performance of more than 4,000 mutual funds sold by financial advisors as compared to those selected by investors on their own between 1996 and 2002. This is the first study ever to scientifically quantify the benefits of using financial advisors, and it appears the authors came up empty-handed!

The tool used to find tangible evidence of a benefit from hiring an advisor was the following set of five questions:

1. Do investors who hire advisors get access to funds that would otherwise be harder to find or evaluate? The answer is yes, but as already noted, *advisor-selected funds under-perform funds that investors select on their own.*[59]

2. Do advisors help clients find funds that are lower cost (excluding distribution costs)? After analyzing several trillion dollars' worth of transactions, the answer is no. In fact, another new study released in late November 2007 by the Zero Alpha Group and Fund Democracy supports this finding. Their study showed that investors who buy index funds through brokers pay half a percentage point more in management fees than do independent investors who go through no-load channels—for essentially the same fund.[60]

3. Do advisors give clients access to funds with better performance? Once again, the answer here is a resounding no. Contrary to everything we are led to believe, the evidence shows that advisors not only under-perform indexes but also under-perform what most people do on their own without an advisor.[61] If that is not a damning indictment, I don't know what is!

4. Do advisors provide superior asset allocation? After years of research covering trillions of dollars of asset allocations, the finding is that advisors do not provide superior asset allocation. They are as likely—possibly even more likely—to get caught up in the hot sector as we are.[62]

5. Do advisors help correct such bad investor behavior as chasing fads and chasing performance? Unfortunately, the answer is no. In fact, the evidence shows that advisors even contribute to such behavior.[63]

Lest you think Bergstresser, Tufano, and Chalmers were biased against advisors, let me set you straight. They went out of their way to give advisors the benefit of the doubt. Not only that, some of the largest and most respected industry groups and research organizations aided the academics in their research.[64]

One final observation worth noting: this study also found that the clients of advisors are less educated than are do-it-yourselfers and have lower net worth than they do.[65] You could certainly make a chicken-and-egg argument here, but let's face facts. Using an advisor to choose your investments is just plain dumb when you can do better on your own.

Trust everybody, but yourself most of all.

—Danish proverb

What does all this mean for you? Get educated about personal finance in general and investing in particular. If you need help, avoid commissioned salespeople like the plague. Seek out someone you can pay a one-time fee to, by the hour, or a retainer if necessary.

No one is going to take care of your money for you. The only person who has no conflict of interest is you. The person best qualified to handle your money is you—or at least you should be. If you are not, you need to get cracking on it right now.

BROKERS

The compensation system for brokers is largely based on trailing commissions, also known as "trailers." These are recurring annual commissions based on the value of assets in products like mutual funds and annuities.

According to a February 17, 2005, *Wall Street Journal* article, Merrill Lynch, Morgan Stanley, and Piper Jaffray have all stopped paying brokers' commissions on smaller accounts.[66] This is because everyone is fighting over the same affluent customers. The big Wall Street firms have little interest in the little guy.

> At Merrill, brokers no longer get paid on accounts with fewer than $50,000 in assets. Previously, brokers were paid 25% of the firm's gross commissions on trades greater than $500 and also got trail fees that came out to 35% of ongoing gross commissions on mutual funds and annuities, among other products. The full-service brokerage house has also pared down broker pay on smaller fee-based accounts.
>
> Morgan Stanley has made similar cuts, as has Piper Jaffray. Clearly, there is now an even greater incentive for brokers at the big Wall Street firms to go after larger accounts and ignore the smaller ones.[67]

So, what is a small account holder to do?

Well, someone wants your business, and that someone is the discount brokerage house. As mentioned in chapter 2, companies like Charles Schwab, Fidelity Investments, E*Trade, TD Ameritrade, optionsXpress,* and Scottrade are actively courting the smaller investor who is no longer of interest to full-service brokers.

Why wait?

It is unlikely you are getting any benefit from being at a full-service firm. You aren't getting individual attention or account management. You are increasingly being handled by a call center and put in boilerplate portfolios. Full-service brokerage firms don't want you because you aren't a profitable account.

Better to switch to a discount brokerage house and learn to manage your account on your own than to let your account languish at a full-service brokerage house that has no financial incentive to give you the time of day.

Whenever I say this on the radio, soon thereafter my inbox is flooded with e-mails from people wanting to leave full-service brokerage firms but finding it too expensive because they have been herded into proprietary and back-end-loaded funds or other investments with steep surrender charges. That is typical. Put you in lousy investments that pay them a lot of money, but make it difficult for you to move yours.

I don't believe you should ever stay in bad investments just because the broker tries to trap you in them. In fact, that is all the more reason to get out. Chalk the cost up to tuition in the college of hard knocks. You will never make the same mistake twice, I guarantee you. Not when it costs you to fix the mistake.

---

*See the appendix for disclosure information regarding optionsXpress.

FINANCIAL PLANNERS

Because of my investment talk show on the radio, I get e-mails like this one on a pretty regular basis.

> *Dear Ms. Snider,*
>
> *My husband and I are in our 50s. Neither one of us has a financial background, and this is a second marriage for both of us. We have only been married for five years. It is PAST time for us to really start financial planning for retirement and thus the reason that your ads have intrigued me.*
>
> *I am not sure where to start. We desperately need to get a retirement plan going. We each have some investments (401[k], husband; IRA, wife) with some money but we need to get much more aggressive in our plan, immediately.*
>
> *I think we need a financial planner (or maybe not) to help us. Someone that we can trust and believe in, and where do we find such a person?????*

Many of you may be thinking about consulting with a financial planner. After all, this market is very confusing. Is this the top, or is the market going higher? How do I provide for my family? How am I ever going to retire? Do I have enough saved to live on? Maybe many of you are already working with a planner.

Do you really need a financial planner? For most people, I believe the answer is no! Very few people need a financial planner because—quite frankly—most of you don't have enough money to require a planner to help you draw up a complicated financial plan. What most people need, instead, are simply education and discipline, and a financial advisor can't and won't give you either one.

I have no problem with the financially educated person who goes to a planner as a partner in the process. This is a person who is educated enough to contribute to the process, to express what he/she specifically wants to achieve, and already has a pretty good idea of how to get there but simply wants a different perspective in case he/she hasn't thought of something.

Where I think people are making a tragic mistake is in substituting an advisor for an education. The thinking goes: "I don't have to really understand this stuff. That's what I pay the advisor for." But again, no one is going to take care of your money for you. The person best qualified to handle your money is you.

If you just automatically rubber-stamp what your advisor proposes, then you have a problem. If you can't have a meaningful conversation with a financial advisor, on an equal footing, about different investments—how they contribute to your objectives, their pros and cons, the costs and implications—then you're not investing. What you're doing is betting: betting that advisors know what they're doing; and betting that they will put your interests before their own. Now, how good a bet do you think that is?

Success is nothing more than a few simple disciplines,
practiced every day.

— Jim Rohn

Here's the other thing I often see. Half the people who e-mail me asking for advice about hiring a financial planner write because they are in trouble. That trouble falls into two categories: bad debt and no retirement savings. Some folks have credit card debt up to their eyeballs, and they want someone to figure out a way to get them out—preferably a painless way in which they don't have to give up anything. Some folks haven't saved enough for retirement, and now with ten years to go before retiring, they are looking for a professional with infinite wisdom and knowledge who can make up for the shortfall of the last 20 years by pulling a rabbit out of a hat.

Well, I have bad news for you. Knowledge alone won't do it. You also have to have discipline, and it is a lack of discipline that got us all into these scrapes in the first place.

Believe me, I know. I have been in every financial mess known to humanity. When I was younger (and, I might add, dumber and more impulsive), I had a boatload of debt. There were long periods in my life during which I had zero savings even though I made a nice income. Retirement planning? Ha! Forget about it!

In fact, many years ago I sought out a CPA in hopes that she could tell me how to bring my expenses in line with my income. When she told me I should start by selling my polo ponies, I fired her! That wasn't what I wanted to hear. I wanted magic, not sacrifice!

In the end, the only way I got out of debt, cleaned up my credit report, and began to put away money to invest was learning to be disciplined. You can know more about investing than anyone else in the whole wide world, but without discipline, that knowledge is useless. It takes discipline—not a financial advisor—to absolve you of your former financial sins. It takes discipline to save, and it takes savings to seed real wealth.

To build financial security requires you to look deep inside yourself and find the discipline of character to exercise sound judgment, moderation, and restraint. This is not an exaggeration. Without those character traits, you will never be financially secure.

By the way, did I mention that discipline is the single hardest part of the investing process? It takes discipline to stay the course. It takes discipline to not get impatient. It takes discipline to not sell every time you get fearful. It takes discipline to not change horses in midstream.

It takes discipline to not buy something you shouldn't because of your greed and avarice. Discipline is an integral part of investing, and no financial planner can create that in you.

While I will concede there are some (maybe even many) good and honest financial planners out there, when someone wants to go visit one, I cringe for three reasons.

1. As I have already discussed, people often seek out planners for the wrong reasons. They are looking for something that needs to be found within themselves, not externally.

2. Most people don't have situations complex enough to warrant hiring a financial advisor. Thus, you're just wasting money if you do. With a little education, you should be able to figure out what you need and then go to individual providers, such as an insurance broker or an attorney, to get the pieces you can't handle yourself.

3. Most financial planners will sell you crap products you don't need.

Financial advisors cloak themselves in respectability by calling themselves financial planners or financial advisors when, in fact, they are simply commissioned salespeople who are paid to sell the mutual fund, stock, annuity, or insurance policy their company wants them to sell. If you go to an advisor with no prior knowledge or understanding, you are then unable to distinguish between a good investment and a good sales pitch. And let me tell you, the good sales pitches outnumber the good investments about a hundred to one. Most of what gets sold is garbage, but you end up buying it because you don't know the difference.

If you doubt me on this, you need only look at the companies involved in recent regulatory investigations, prosecutions, and settlements. You would be hard-pressed to find a large financial services company that has not been implicated in the fleecing of investors. They include, but are not limited to: Merrill Lynch, Morgan Stanley, Bear Stearns, CS First Boston, Goldman Sachs, Lehman, JP Morgan, Citigroup, Solomon Smith Barney, UBS Warburg, Charles Schwab, TD Waterhouse, Edward Jones, Piper Jaffray, Putnam, Strong, Scudder, Janus, Alliance Federated, Franklin Templeton, INVESCO, PIMCO, Bank of America, Bank One, Waddell & Reed, Prudential, Wachovia . . . I could keep going because this is just a partial list. You get the point?

If you really do think you need a planner, then by all means, make sure you work exclusively with a fee-only financial planner. A fee-only financial planner is one who gets paid by the hour or as a percentage of the assets they manage for you rather than by accepting commissions on the products they sell you. That is the only way you can know the planner will have no conflict of interest.

You may hear some people use the term *fee-based*. Don't be fooled. Fee-based financial planners and fee-only financial planners are not the same thing. Fee-based firms take your money and their commissions! Make sure your planner is fee only.

One way to find a fee-only planner is through the National Association of Personal Financial Advisors (NAPFA). For a planner to be a member of NAPFA, they must be fee only. NAPFA has a search tool on its Web site for locating fee-only planners in your area. That Web address is www.napfa.org.

If you are working with an advisor now, or you're thinking about working with one in the near future, my advice would be to stop for a minute and ask yourself why. What is your reason for seeking out help? If it is because you don't know enough or because you hope someone else will instill the discipline to get you out of a mess, you might want to rethink your situation.

Best-selling author and financial journalist Jane Bryant Quinn puts it this way in *Making the Most of Your Money:* "Most of us don't need professional planners. We don't even need a full-scale plan. Conservative money management isn't hard. To be your own guru, you need only a list of objectives, a few simple financial products, realistic investment expectations, a time frame that gives your investments time to work out, and a well-tempered humbug detector, to keep you from falling for rascally sales pitches."[68]

chapter 14

CREATE PASSIVE INCOME

You can shear a sheep many times, but you can only sell it once.
—Vermont Proverb

I BELIEVE WE ARE in the midst of an inevitable shift in the investment model. We are moving from a model in which our lifetime investment objective is accumulation to one in which our lifetime investment objective is income generation. Such a shift requires us to retool old thinking—something that is never easy and may be impossible for some.

The accumulation model is a race against time. We measure success in the accumulation model by our performance: a number, our net asset value at any one point in time. The goal is for the market value of your portfolio to be as high as possible at all times. In particular, we are working toward the net asset value at two different artificial milestones.

The first milestone is the day you retire. The assumption is that as you approach retirement, you will convert larger and larger percentages of your assets to income-producing ones. If you are going to convert them over time—in other words, sell them so you can replace them with assets that accomplish a different goal—the market value at the time of conversion is very important. It is devastating to your lifetime net worth to sell assets when their value is sharply depressed because you have to.

The second milestone is the day you die. The assumption here is that on the day you die, whatever you have left will pass to your heirs.

Previous generations were not concerned with either of these two milestones. As I mentioned briefly in chapter 2, great-grandparents worked all their lives, then they died. The life expectancy after age 65 was short. If they happened to outlive the normal life expectancy, their family cared for them. What our great-grandparents passed to our grandparents, who in turn passed to our parents, was, in all likelihood, not money or securities but possessions: their house, land, businesses, furniture, jewelry, and family heirlooms.

In 1965, stock market investments were rare. Less than 10 percent of Americans owned common stock.[69] Most of our parents were guaranteed a lifetime income by military and employer pension plans and Social Security. Even as the life expectancy lengthened, healthcare was affordable and provided by retiree health benefits and Medicare.

Our world changed significantly in 1974 when Congress passed the Employee Retirement Income Security Act, better known as ERISA. Contrary to its name, ERISA began the process wherein the burden and risk of providing retirement income shifted away from employers and onto employees. ERISA began the inexorable shift from a certain, if modest, retirement income to an uncertain future based on high-risk stock market investments in 401(k) plans and IRAs.

Accumulation using diversified high-risk investments came into being not because it was the best alternative but because it was the *only* alternative. The sole way to guarantee a secure retirement was to work for 40 years during the prime of your life, at something you didn't necessarily enjoy, so you could accumulate enough money that you could maintain a decent lifestyle for an indefinite period of time on safe but low bond yields.

It doesn't have to be that way anymore. And it shouldn't. The Internet, democratization of the financial markets, and financial engineering have all brought about game-changing shifts in the way we can and should invest. Because we have cheap and real-time access to information and to markets that 20 years ago were reserved strictly for institutional investors, new and better ways to meet lifetime investment objectives are coming to market on a daily basis.

This brings us to the reemergence of the income-generation model. Only in the last few years have financial engineers devised new and better ways of generating higher than bond market yields with reasonable levels of risk.

I say reemergence because the income-generation model is not new. It is a throwback to the days of our grandparents. But, as the old car ad said, "This is not your father's Oldsmobile." The income-generation model is about outcomes instead of numbers and artificial milestones. It is about creating a real and increasing cash flow over your lifetime. Success for income investors is the amount and consistency of that periodic paycheck generated by their portfolio instead of by their labor.

The market value of their portfolio is not a primary concern for income investors. They have a luxury that accumulation or growth investors do not. Income investors don't have to concern themselves with temporary losses in value, only with permanent ones. This is indeed a luxury given that there is no way to avoid short-term, unrealized losses of capital except by putting your money in CDs, savings accounts, or treasure chests you bury in the backyard. The market value of all investments fluctuates commensurate with the level of return. The higher the return, the more fluctuation in market value. The lower the return, the less fluctuation.

In trying to mitigate short-term market risk, accumulation investors achieve the opposite result—the Performance Paradox I mentioned
in chapter 12. Accumulation investors keep score by trying to maintain
an ever-increasing net asset value, and they try to outsmart the market
by timing. Unfortunately, the academic evidence tells us markets cannot be timed and stocks cannot be picked successfully over long periods
of time.

The focus on net asset value for accumulation investors achieves
the opposite result from what they seek. Over the 20-year period ending in 2006, the S&P 500 was up an average of 11.8 percent.[70] U.S.
stock mutual funds had a return over the same period of 10.6 percent.[71]
Even professional mutual fund managers cannot beat the market by
picking stocks. The stock mutual fund investor had a return of only 2.7
percent,[72] which goes to show that investors who try to pick funds or
time the market do so at their own peril.

As I said previously, the objective of the income investor is to generate the biggest paycheck possible from his portfolio with the least
amount of risk. I will talk about how that is accomplished in a moment,
but for now, let's just assume that it can be done. Income investing
provides for all of the outcomes the accumulation investor is seeking
while removing some of the potential pitfalls and offering additional
benefits as well.

We have this idea that growth and income objectives are mutually
exclusive. If my portfolio generates income, or yield, at the rate of 8 to
10 percent a year, and I don't need that money, I reinvest it to create
what? Growth!

Typically, in an income portfolio the cash flow is a function of the
amount invested, not the market value of the underlying assets. For
example, say I buy $100,000 of bonds paying 5 percent. My income,
or cash flow, would be $5,000 a year, regardless of the market value of

those bonds over time. Whether they are up or down, my income, so long as the bond issuer doesn't default, is unchanged.

Again, imagine I don't need the $5,000 a year because I am still working and receiving a W-2 paycheck. I use the income to buy more bonds. As a result, my monthly income goes up. Even if the value of my bonds declines, my income is growing.

People seem to me to be happiest when they are working for nothing and can afford to do so.

—Robert Lynd

To me, the true measure of wealth is not the size of the portfolio, as measured by its net asset value, but its ability to support a sustainable lifestyle indefinitely into the future. If this is the case, you can then see, by extension, that income portfolios (which generate cash flow as a percentage of the investment, not the current asset value) are for the most part impervious to market declines, so long as the investor has a reasonably long-term time horizon. As I said earlier, your time horizon is the whole of your life expectancy. More accurately for couples, it is the joint life expectancy of you and your spouse.

A portfolio that generates a reliable and consistent cash flow is much more flexible than a portfolio aimed at some future date. What happens if you need that money sooner? What happens if your future date comes at the wrong time? Conversion, in either case, can be crippling.

However, if I already have a portfolio that is generating enough cash flow to pay my bills, and that cash flow is growing by at least the average rate of inflation, should I lose my job or become disabled, I don't have to worry about converting to income-producing assets at a time when the market may be down. My portfolio already creates cash flow. Rather than reinvesting it, I now begin to spend it.

There are five ways to generate passive income, or cash flow.

RENT—This is money received when you rent out real property, such as a house or an apartment. Many successful cash flow investors use real estate to create passive income. I just don't happen to be one of them. Real estate has never been my thing.

ROYALTIES—This is passive income received from the licensing of intellectual property. Examples would include a screenplay, a piece of software, a song . . . or a book.

DIVIDENDS—This is passive income received as a result of the distribution of profits to shareholders.

INTEREST—This is passive income paid by a borrower as compensation for money you loaned.

OPTION PREMIUM—This is passive income received from the sale of options against an asset. This is my personal favorite. The beauty of option premium to create cash flow is its flexibility. Rather than accepting the going rate of interest or dividend yield, I can structure my investment to fall at the point along the risk-reward continuum that fits my investment profile.

Gradually, more and more people are waking up to reality. That reality for many in the wave of 80 million baby boomers who will begin to retire in 2008 is their lack of savings and their need for income.

An article in the March 21, 2005, issue of *Barron's* newsweekly, titled "Income to Spare,"[73] looks at most of the income-producing investments including some pretty obscure ones few people know about. Of course, they left one out. The Snider Investment Method®* wasn't in that list, but I am sure that was just an unintended oversight on the part of the writer!

---

*See the appendix for disclosures related to the Snider Investment Method® and the Snider Investment Method Workshop.

Here are some of the income-producing investments listed in the *Barron's* article. (Note that all yields are effective as of February 1, 2008, and have been obtained from sources deemed to be reliable. These yields will change significantly over time.)

DIVIDEND-PAYING STOCKS—The dividend yield on the S&P 500 is currently at 2.1 percent.[74] You can find some companies paying some pretty decent dividends. *Barron's* had a chart of 26 companies with dividend yields of 3.5 percent or higher that had increased their dividends for at least ten years in a row and had consistent earnings.[75] But to create a diversified portfolio, you will have to settle for something close to the average.

ETFS ON DIVIDEND INDEX—These exchange-traded funds, based on the indexes of dividend-paying stocks, are yielding 3.22 percent,[76] lower than many of the stocks themselves but an easy way to play dividends.

MUTUAL FUND OF DIVIDEND STOCKS—The managers of these funds focus on total return, not just yield, so the yields tend to be pretty puny at 1.91 percent.[77]

MUNICIPAL BONDS—Average yield on AAA-rated 15-year municipal bonds is 3.84 percent,[78] and it is exempt from federal taxes. You probably wouldn't want to put these in your IRA since they are already tax deferred, but they can be a good way to shelter taxable yield from Uncle Sam if you are in a high tax bracket.

EMERGING MARKET DEBT—If you want to take on some risk in your income portfolio, these may be just the ticket. The current yield on a sampling of emerging market bond funds ranged between 5 and 8 percent.[79]

REITS—Real estate investment trusts must pay 90 percent of their income to shareholders in the form of a dividend. The yield on REITs is averaging 4.12 percent.[80]

CDs—Certificates of deposit are issued by banks and are FDIC insured. A five-year CD paid anywhere from a low of 3.49 percent to a high of 5.1 percent in 2007.[81] Shorter maturities pay less.

CANADIAN ROYALTY TRUSTS (CANROYs)—Similar to REITs, which are based on real estate, royalty trusts pay out cash flows from oil and gas and other commodity properties. Be aware that these do not work like bonds. They are also subject to serious legislative risk, as the Canadian government—home to many royalty trusts—recently changed the law. Beginning in 2011, CANROYs will no longer be tax advantaged. It is likely that the yield on Canadian trusts will drop down to the 2 to 4 percent range. For now, though, the yield is high. A sampling of the yield of CANROYs that trade on American stock exchanges ranged from 11 to 15 percent.[82] Note that because there is no return of principal, the total return may be quite low.

TIPS—Treasury inflation-protected securities are U.S. Treasury bonds that adjust the principal with moves in the consumer price index. Right now, TIPS maturing in 2032 are paying a guaranteed 1.62 percent,[83] and they will be adjusted for inflation over time.

While the following income-producing investments weren't mentioned in the article, I think they should have been:

OPTION INCOME CLOSED-END FUNDS—These are mutual funds that trade on an exchange and have the production of income from the sale of options as their investment objective. These funds have proliferated in recent years and typically yield between 8 and 10 percent.

THE SNIDER INVESTMENT METHOD®—My proprietary method of generating portfolio income had an average yield of 13.3 percent for the period from September 2002 through February 2008. The risk of permanent loss of capital is commensurate with an equity investment.*

Many of these topics, including the creation of passive income, are so big that I could write an entire book on them. Maybe someday I will.

---

*See the appendix for disclosures related to the Snider Investment Method® and the Snider Investment Method Workshop.

In the meantime, however, simply remember our goal: To always have enough money to do what we want, when we want, without worrying how to pay for it. Income that you don't have to work for is the best way to permanently achieve that goal.

chapter 15

CONTROL WHAT YOU CAN; IGNORE THE REST

Risk is the chance of loss, and for most of history it was viewed as that. There is a chance I'm going to lose. But in the capitalist system, risk is also an opportunity. Nothing ventured, nothing gained is as important to keep in mind as the fear that if I don't manage my affairs, I can get wiped out.
—Peter Bernstein

YOU CANNOT CONTROL THE business cycle, stock prices, bond yields, inflation, or the dollar. You cannot control who gets elected president or which party controls Congress. You cannot control wars or terrorists. One key to financial success is to control the things you can—and to ignore the rest.

RISK

Managing risk can be a very complex subject if you want it to be. Massive texts have been written about managing risk. College courses are offered about managing risk. Ph.D. candidates write their dissertations about managing risk. Harry Markowitz won a Nobel Prize for diversification, a novel concept (at the time) about how to manage risk. You can enroll in classes on non-correlated assets, beta, hedging strategies—all kinds of things.

But to me, the issue is much simpler than that. If you want to manage risk, stay away from risky investments. What are risky investments? I define risky investments as anything that bets on the future direction of prices. In my playbook, that includes owning individual stocks, stock indexes, or mutual funds with the idea that I can buy them for one price and sell them for more, later on, to a greater fool. The same holds true for trying to flip condos in Florida or betting on currency or commodity prices.

All of these are a bet on a random event. I don't see them as any different from betting on the ponies, buying lottery tickets, or playing slots in Las Vegas.

Personally, I will put my hard-earned money in only a very few places. The bulk of Jim's and my total investable assets (excluding our equity in real estate and our business) is in the Snider Investment Method®.* The remainder includes our emergency fund, of course; some money in qualified retirement plans; money needed for something specific within the next two years; or accounts that are too small to be invested using the Snider Investment Method®. All of that money sits in a savings account, money market funds, T-bills, or laddered CDs. I would own U.S. Treasury bonds and TIPS as well, but at the moment we don't.

---

*See the appendix for disclosures related to the Snider Investment Method® and the Snider Investment Method Workshop

*In investing money, the amount of interest you want should
depend on whether you want to eat well or sleep well.*

—J. Kenfield Morley

In the past, I have spoken to groups and on my radio show about the differences between institutional investors and retail investors. One of the key differences between the two groups is that institutional investors focus on risk, whereas retail investors focus on performance. Institutional investors spend their days measuring and minimizing risk. They know that if they manage risk properly, the return will be there. Retail investors spend their days chasing after a bigger number.

Retail investors think that what institutional investors do is boring. They think they cannot possibly live on low-risk returns. They are wrong. They cannot possibly live on high-risk returns.

Again, you will recall that retail stock mutual fund investors have had an average return of only 4.3 percent per year over the 20 years ending in 2006. The reason retail investors do so poorly is because they insist on chasing performance.

Please note that I am using stock mutual funds to make this point because we have empirical data from Dalbar that measure the effects. But the same is true of all speculation, whether on stocks, real estate, commodities, or casino games.

Pigs get fat, but hogs get slaughtered.

For my radio show, I had the pleasure of interviewing Terry Burnham, Harvard economics professor and author of *Mean Markets and*

Lizard Brains. The term *lizard brain* comes from the field of neuroeconomics: that is, the study of how our brain function affects financial decision making.

In that interview, Professor Burnham advised everyone to cut their risk by one-half to three-quarters. You might be asking yourself, "How can he say that when he has no idea how much risk I'm taking today?"

He can say that without knowing how much risk you're actually taking because he *does* know that your lizard brain—all of our lizard brains—cause us to underestimate risk. Cutting the amount of risk *you think you can take* in half will be about the amount *you should be taking*!

Investing isn't supposed to be exciting, and it isn't supposed to be time-consuming. Not if you do it right. Investors would be far better served if they abandoned this fool's errand they are on and started focusing on avoiding permanent losses (as distinguished from short-term fluctuations in asset prices) and generating positive cash flow on a consistent monthly basis. That way, no matter what happens, they can still live in the manner to which they have become accustomed. That is how I manage risk. You can become such an investor too.

EXPENSES

Everybody focuses a lot of time and attention on minimizing taxes. But guess what? The biggest drain on your returns isn't taxes; it's the fees and commissions being collected by those same advisors who are talking about all those nasty taxes. The fact is that you'll pay four times more to your fund manager than you will to Uncle Sam in taxes. How, you might ask.

This example will illustrate how. Suppose you and your spouse don't have any dependents when you reach retirement. You're at that $1 million mark and you decide you can live off $40,000 a year. And suppose the $40,000 is ordinary income, so, rather than itemizing your deductions, you'll just take the standard deduction on your tax return. The government gets around $4,000, but your money manager will get *four times* that amount.

You see, the fund industry gets about 1.52 percent in expenses from you (weighted expense ratio with ten-year amortization of sales loads), the consumer, in order to pay for things like marketing, taxes, tools, and the occasional piece of advice.[84] You and your spouse will be paying your friendly fund manager $15,200 every year based on your $1 million portfolio. That's *four times* what you're paying in federal taxes! And for what? Certainly not for performance, since two-thirds of all actively managed funds under-perform the benchmark indexes.[85]

Now let's pretend you and your spouse have an investment advisor in addition to your mutual fund manager, and he/she's convinced you to wrap up your retirement assets in a high-commission insurance product like a variable annuity. Remember that expense ratio of 1.52? Well, it could climb to as much as 2.50 percent—or more!

Now you and your partner are paying an outlandish $25,000 a year to your fund manager and advisor to manage a portfolio that could be managed by you, with better results, for next to nothing. $25,000 is more than *half* of what you've taken out to live on every year. I don't know about you, but I think retirement is supposed to be fun and engaging, and I could have a lot more fun on $65,000 than I could on $40,000.

The saddest part is that that $25,000 figure is about $20,000 more than what you really have to pay. Why do brokers and financial advisors continue to harp on taxes? It's a canard—a diversion—to keep us from focusing on their fees, and we fall for it.

Believe me, I'm not pointing a finger at you. Remember, I went from rags to riches back to rags in less than two years because I didn't know what was going on in my portfolio. Like many of you, I trusted my broker to handle my money partly because I believed that he was more qualified than I was to do it. That assumption cost me a whole lot of money.

The fastest way to improve the returns in your portfolio without taking on one ounce of additional risk is to lower your fees. The best way to lower your fees is to ditch your money managers. You don't need them, and in spite of what you might think, you don't need to spend countless hours in order to manage your own money.

YOUR EMOTIONS

Remember that in chapter 11 I spoke about ignoring and curbing your emotional responses? The most difficult thing about investing is that, as humans, we have emotions. Those emotions come from our lizard brains. And, as Harvard Professor Burnham points out, our lizard brains are screwing us up. A related field to neuroeconomics is that of behavioral finance. This is the psychology of investing. The field of behavioral finance was born in the 1970s, after researchers discovered that the stock market's volatility was due in large part to investors' emotional reactions to prices. Today, groups of academics meet regularly and publish widely on the subject of emotional investing. In fact, the 2002 Nobel Prize in economic sciences was awarded, in part, to Daniel Kahneman, a professor of psychology at Princeton University, for "having integrated insights from psychological research into economic science, especially concerning human judgment and decision making under uncertainty."

Emotions—predominantly greed—are to blame for the recent mutual fund scandals, and they are to blame for every market bubble, from the tulip craze of the 1630s to the Internet craze of the 1990s. So long as humans are doing the investing, emotions will be involved. As an investor, you want to limit your emotional reactions. You can do this by understanding that you have psychological biases that keep you emotionally wound up.

I have interviewed any number of experts in the field of behavioral finance for my radio show. Along with Dr. Burnham, the list includes Michael Brennan, Robert Shiller, and John Nofsinger. Dr. Nofsinger says that our brains couldn't survive on logic alone; our brains need emotion.[86] For example, how many times have you instantly taken a liking or disliking to someone without knowing him/her well, only to find out your hunch was right? Emotions play a big role in our survival. They are quite useful in many aspects of our everyday lives, but they are quite detrimental when it comes to our investments. Here's why.

Again, as discussed in chapter 11, we know that our brains naturally take shortcuts, called heuristics, in order to arrive at a decision. These shortcuts are, in fact, necessary in order for us to get by each day. Imagine how laborious life would be if you had to contemplate the pros and cons of iceberg lettuce over spinach. Unfortunately, taking these shortcuts isn't a good practice when you're investing. Choosing iceberg over spinach doesn't carry the same consequences as choosing how much to invest or what to invest in. Heuristic investors thwart the pros-versus-cons process and make a final judgment based on how they feel. This kind of investor tends to badly distort the likelihood of gain or loss and to grossly underestimate risk.

A second psychological bias is familiarity bias. According to Dr. Nofsinger, human beings tend to think that those stocks or companies with which we are familiar are better or safer than those with which we are unfamiliar. The familiarity bias accounts for all those people who have left their money at a full-service brokerage firm, or a tainted fund company, even though they know, logically, that they are being screwed. It is a classic case of the devil you know being less scary than the devil you don't. That familiarity could be personal too. Are you staying with a stock because you play golf with the president of the company?

A third type of psychological bias is called representative bias. When the market goes up, investors feel better about the funds they are in or the stocks they have purchased. Studies show that investors automatically assume they are getting as good as or better than the market return even though most of them are not.

I asked Dr. Nofsinger what I could do to help investors remember—even though the market may rally, even though they may see short-term gains, and even though they may like their mutual fund manager or broker—how unhappy they are when they are losing money and to compel them to make the switch to a saner way of investing.

He rattled off three things, the first of which is to control your environment. If you were starting a new low-carb diet, you wouldn't stock your fridge with bread and potatoes, would you? Watching CNBC, reading all the financial magazines, and—worst of all—checking the stock market every day is like stocking the fridge. It sets you up for an emotional reaction. When stocks are down, you are down, and you want to quickly sell them so you can cut your losses. But if you do, you'll get hit with fees and commissions, you'll lose more money, and you'll typically just jump right back into another "hot" stock that won't turn out to be so hot after all.

During the November 2003 Seventh Congress on Psychology and Investing (sponsored by the Continuing Education Program, Inc., at the Massachusetts Mental Health Center—a teaching hospital of Harvard Medical School—and Trend Reflection Investment Software), scientists released a study showing that the reaction of investors to a loss is intensified if they also experienced a recent loss in their personal life. What happens in our home life has a direct correlation to our investing decisions. Even simple chemical responses like being hungry can affect our investment decisions. Someone who has recently retired or has been laid off, for example, has many investment decisions to make, just at the time they are most vulnerable to making bad ones. Control your environment and you will automatically make better decisions.

The second thing investors can do is to understand the different types of psychological biases they can have. I have named three—shortcuts, familiarity, representative—but there are quite a few others. Before acting on a decision, ask yourself whether that decision is a reaction caused by one of the biases. Remember the motto of the cartoon character GI Joe: Knowing is half the battle. He's right. If you are aware of these tendencies, then you will be more likely to control them.

The third and final thing you can do is form a plan. It sounds deceptively simple, but forming a plan is the first step toward rational investing. A very simple plan, for example, would be to place trades on the first of the month—never any other day—no matter what was happening. This would force you to consider your decisions longer and more carefully rather than making an off-the-cuff decision. All the studies show that even something this simple can actually improve your results dramatically. Whether your plan simply sets minimal criteria or uses a more robust model like our Snider Investment Method®,* formulate that plan and stick to it. It's not a magic pill, but it will help you stay sane while you're growing your wealth.

---

*While the model might be robust, performance is not guaranteed. See the appendix for disclosures related to the Snider Investment Method® and the Snider Investment Method Workshop.

chapter 16

DON'T LET THE TAX TAIL WAG THE INVESTMENT DOG

The only thing that hurts more than paying an income tax is not having to pay an income tax.
—Lord Dewar

YOUR BOSS CALLS YOU into his office. "Jones, you've done great work for the company. We're going to promote you. Your salary will double over what you're making now. So, do you want the job?"

"Gee, I don't know," you reply. "Let me have a little while to think about it."

As you walk back to your office, you start to think about all the things you've been putting off that doubling your salary would let you afford. You've been waiting to finish the new deck. You and your spouse are in dire need of a vacation. And you know you need to get going on your kid's college education fund. All of these are now possible given the salary you've been offered.

But before you call home with the good news, you sit down and do some calculations. Your income right now is $80,000 a year. You are paying about $9,500 a year in taxes, leaving you with about $70,500 after taxes. When you look at your new salary, you see that you will be paying about $30,300 a year in taxes, leaving you with just a little less than $130,000.

You walk into your boss's office and tell him, "Sorry, sir, but I don't want the job."

"What? Why not? This is a great opportunity for you."

"It is, sir, and I really appreciate your faith in me. It's just that I don't want to pay the taxes on the increase."

You would never do this, right? It's absurd. Yes, your effective tax rate has jumped from 11.5 to 19 percent, and the actual dollars you are paying in taxes have increased, but so has your net income after tax. Who cares that you are paying more in taxes?

Yet, many people do exactly this when it comes to their investments. I call this "letting the tax tail wag the investment dog," and nine times out of ten, it is an investor train wreck waiting to happen.

The tax tail wagging the investment dog usually takes one of three forms. The first is the person who holds on to an appreciated security to avoid paying the capital gains tax. The second is the person who chooses a terrible investment over a better one because the bad one is tax deferred. The third is the person who holds on to cash because they don't want to pay the taxes on any gains they make if they invest it.

When I am giving speeches, one of the questions I often ask the audience is, "How many of you are holding on to stocks that were once profitable but now are underwater?" Always there are groans, and at least half of the people in the room raise their hand. Then I ask those men and women, "How many of you didn't sell them because you wanted to wait at least a year from when you bought them in order to get the cheaper long-term capital gains rate?" Not all, but many of the hands stay up.

Unfortunately, stock prices don't watch the calendar. They don't know how long you've owned them, and usually, they don't wait until it's convenient for you before they head back down again. When a stock hits your target price, you have to sell, tax consequences be darned. One of the most common investor mistakes is turning a winner into a loser, and often the rationale is taxes.

Now, as much as I hate it when I see someone do this, I can at least understand it. What we're dealing with is an unknown: namely, the future price of the stock. And we are, by nature, optimistic, so we always think our stocks will keep going up. What I absolutely cannot understand, however, is the person who chooses to put money in a variable or equity index annuity to avoid taxes. Well, I take that back. I do understand it. Most investors are lied to about what they should expect from their annuities.

We know that variable annuities are terrible investments that don't do anywhere near as well as the market overall. We also know that when you cash out of an annuity, the gains will be taxed as ordinary income, not as capital gains. Let me give you a real-life example. I received an e-mail the other day from a gentleman who put $200,000 in an annuity 18 years ago. Over that time period, his investment has doubled. That is about a 4 percent return over 18 years. If he cashes out, he will pay 35 percent on a $200,000 gain, or $70,000.

Now, let's suppose that instead of that annuity, he had just put his money in an S&P 500 index fund 18 years ago and hadn't touched it since. Instead of a 4 percent return, he would have an annualized return of 11.25 percent per year, for a gain of $676,333 (rather than $200,000). He would pay long-term capital gains taxes of 15 percent, or $101,450, leaving him with an after-tax gain of $574,883!

This gentleman was looking at the Snider Investment Method® because he was intrigued by the yield,* but he doesn't want to pay the tax on the gains in the annuity. The only way he can avoid that tax is by

---

*See the appendix for disclosures related to the Snider Investment Method® and the Snider Investment Method Workshop.

leaving it in the annuity. So, he will settle—and I do mean settle—for 4 percent a year. This is why I call annuities the "Hotel California" of investment products: once you get in, you can never get out—at least, not without some pain.

Imagine he cashes out the annuity, invests the $330,000 left after taxes in an S&P 500 index fund, and makes an average return of 10 percent over ten years. Ten years later that $330,000 is approximately $856,000 before tax.

If, however, he leaves the $400,000 in the annuity, doesn't pay the taxes, and continues to earn 4 percent, his $400,000 is only $592,000 before tax. And eventually, he will still have to pay the tax! This example is just like turning down the job offer because of the additional taxes.

On a more personal level, Jim and I have a family friend who literally has millions of dollars *in cash*. We have approached him several times about investing that money, or at least some of that money, even if it is just putting it in something safe that pays more than a savings account. He has declined, saying that if he took our advice, he would have to pay taxes on any gains!

This is not a dumb man. He made that money; it was not handed to him. He knows that inflation eats away at that money by about 3 percent each year. Still, he would rather lose purchasing power than pay taxes—even on a perfectly safe investment like U.S. Treasury bonds!

Sometimes in this business, all I can do is just shake my head.

I am proud to be paying taxes in the United States.
The only thing is, I could be just as proud for half the money.
—Arthur Godfrey

We have been brainwashed by the financial services industry to think of taxes as the great evil that eats away at our nest egg. In fact, the amount we pay in fees dwarfs what we pay in capital gains taxes. It is one of the world's greatest diversionary tactics, and it has worked so well that people now do silly, silly things just to avoid taxes.

I take the opposite approach. I pay a lot of taxes. A lot of taxes! I hope I have to pay a lot of taxes for the rest of my life. Now don't get me wrong; I don't pay any more than I have to. But paying taxes means I am making a lot of money, and money is what pays for outcomes—the outcomes I defined as my money's higher purpose back in chapter 10.

So when you find yourself getting all twisted up about taxes, ask yourself, "Am I letting the tax tail wag the investment dog?"

chapter 17

IGNORE INFLATION AT YOUR PERIL

It's a great country, but you can't live in it for nothing.
—Will Rogers

AS I MENTIONED EARLIER, I went to the University of Colorado (go Buffs!), also known as "Ski-U." Freshman year, my ski days numbered in the triple digits, if that gives you any indication of my priorities. And no, I wasn't on the ski team. Back then, we could buy books of coupons good for discounts on food, lodging, and lift passes at ski areas all over the state. I could ski the top-notch areas like Aspen or Vail for less than $20 a day.

Recently, I read an article that said lift passes at many of the big ski areas are now approaching $100 a day![87] This is why I believe inflation, not market losses, is the biggest threat to your wealth.

Since my college days in the early '80s, the price of a lift ticket has gone up an average of about 6.5 percent per year. That is faster than the rate of inflation overall, which averages roughly 3 percent per year.

Now, imagine that my fixed income as a college student is $100 a month. Back in 1985, I was living large on that $100: I could ski anywhere, for an entire weekend, on less than that—gas, food, and lodging included. (Granted, I wasn't staying at the Four Seasons, but still!)

Today, assuming my income wasn't being adjusted by at least the rate of inflation, I could barely afford a one-day lift pass. My income of $100 hasn't changed, but my purchasing power is sharply diminished.

A friend of mine asked me why anyone would invest in stocks. She has all of her money in bonds paying 5 percent. There is almost no risk, and the income produced is enough to pay all of her bills . . . today! She thinks that as long as she takes out only the 5 percent each year when she retires, she can live indefinitely on that money. What she isn't accounting for is—you guessed it—inflation.

So, let's calculate how much you really need in order to stay ahead of the inflation bogey monster. Suppose you spend 4 percent of the value of your portfolio each year, after tax, in retirement. Assume a 25 percent marginal tax bracket and a 3.5 percent average annual rate of inflation. You would need a gross average annualized return of 10 percent ($[4 + 3.5] \div [1 - .25]$).

Over the last ten years, the U.S. bond market total return has been approximately 5.5 percent. Clearly, a bond portfolio falls woefully short. Unless you are Warren Buffett—in other words, a billionaire with a reasonably modest standard of living—you are going to have to generate something significantly higher than bond market returns in order to sustain a reasonable standard of living once you start living off the proceeds of your portfolio.

So, while we would all like to stop worrying about the market's ups and downs and retreat to the so-called safe havens offered by lower-return investments as we get older, our reality requires us to do two things: (1) construct your portfolio so that the returns are high enough to sustain both growth and a reasonable standard of living; and (2) avoid the mistakes that cause investor return to be lower than invest-ment return. In a very real sense, your success as an investor will depend on your ability to tolerate the short-term fluctuations that come with higher-return investments.

These stock market fluctuations are nothing to be afraid of. We ex-perience fluctuations every day. Weather fluctuates. The performance of our favorite athlete or team fluctuates. Prices fluctuate. We don't think of these as risks, and we certainly don't avoid shopping or going to the ballpark because of fear of fluctuations.

The real risk is running out of money while you are still alive. Or not reaching the goals that are most important to you. Stock market fluctuations are not the bogeyman standing between you and your goals—inflation is. Make sure you are not fighting the wrong dragon.

SECTION FIVE

Manage Risk

chapter 18

KNOW YOUR
GREATEST RISK

It does not do to leave a live dragon
out of your calculations, if you live near him.
—J. R. R. Tolkien

WHAT IS YOUR MOST valuable asset? Your business? Your house? Your investment portfolio? Your pile of gold buried in your backyard? What would you guess?

If you guessed anything tangible, you guessed wrong. Your most valuable asset is what economists call your human capital. This is the sum total of the skills, knowledge, and wisdom you possess and then trade with your employer or your customers for money. When you are young, human capital represents the lion's share of your total wealth. As you age and begin to accumulate other assets, human capital represents a smaller proportion of your total wealth, but it is still your largest asset.

If that is so, and economists tell us it is, then your biggest risk is not being sued if someone slips and falls in your driveway, a protracted bear market, or the cost of long-term healthcare. Your biggest risk is disability or obsolescence. Both have the potential to seriously disrupt your income.

Think of it. As long as my income stream keeps flowing, I can get through almost everything else. Suppose someone does slip and fall in my driveway. That person sues me and is awarded millions of dollars in a court judgment. I may have to file for bankruptcy, but the court will allow me to retain enough of my income to keep a roof over my head and to feed and clothe my family.

Imagine our society experiences an economic depression so severe that stock prices take 30 years to recover. As long as I don't lose my job and I can still work, I can still eat.

Imagine I work in a family business that continues to pay me long after I have become old and feeble. Long-term healthcare is not a problem.

I am not saying life would be champagne and caviar. I am just saying it would be better than the alternative. A steady income solves many problems. Loss of one can wreak havoc.

DISABILITY

We have two choices when it comes to risk. We can either hedge it or insure it. Insuring a risk is almost always more costly than hedging it because the intermediaries—namely, insurance companies—have to make a profit over and above the cost of the hedge.

From fortune to misfortune is but a step; from misfortune to fortune is a long way.

—Yiddish proverb

We can insure the risk of disability by purchasing disability insurance. Some employers offer disability insurance as an employee benefit. Disability policies can be either short term or long term.

Short-term disability policies pay you a percentage of your salary if you are temporarily unable to work because of injury or illness. A typical policy will pay you anywhere from 50 to 65 percent of your pay for anywhere from 2 weeks to 2 years, depending on the policy you purchase. A period of 13 to 26 weeks is more common, and then long-term disability kicks in if you have it.

Long-term disability replaces income for a much longer period of time. Policies usually limit benefits to 5 years or age 65, whichever comes first.

Of course, being the optimists that we are, no one likes to think about what happens if disaster strikes. But the question asked by a family CFO most often has to be, "What if . . ."

Data from the American Council of Life Insurers tells us one in seven will experience a disability lasting more than five years. The odds increase to one in five for those of us between the ages of 35 and 65.[88] It turns out the leading cause of disabilities is not freak accidents, as many people think, but devastating illnesses such as cancer or heart disease. The long-term loss of income is so disruptive that 46 percent of home foreclosures are due to medical disability.[89]

OBSOLESCENCE

You cannot insure against obsolescence, but you can hedge against the risk. How? By making constant upgrades to the software between your ears. The best hedge against being replaced by a 23-year-old whiz kid is lifelong learning.

---

*Those who do not read are no better off
than those who cannot.*

—Proverb

Lifelong learning need not be formal to be effective. Several years ago, I had the pleasure of interviewing Dr. Benoît Mandelbrot for my radio show. Dr. Mandelbrot, Sterling Professor of Mathematical Sciences, Emeritus, at Yale University, is best known as the father of fractal geometry. Fractal geometry is what makes the stunning reality of modern-day computer animation possible.

His accomplishments are unique in that he has been awarded major prizes not just in mathematics but also in physics, medicine, science, and technology. His concepts have also been applied to economics, earth sciences, and linguistics.

Dr. Mandelbrot credits his ability to think outside the traditional confines of a single branch of science to his unconventional education. "To tell the truth, and not to sound pretentious, but circumstances prevented me from acquiring a real college or university education in the traditional sense, so I am primarily self taught."[90]

PASSIVE INCOME

Disability and obsolescence can both be hedged by building a portfolio that produces enough passive income to pay all the bills, as described in chapter 14. When passive income equals or exceeds day-to-day living expenses, work is no longer a necessity; it is a choice.

Jim and I use a combination of passive income and disability insurance to hedge our risk. Because I am the public face of our company, if

I were to become disabled, our business would be seriously impacted. But we still have employees and bills to pay.

We have a disability policy on me that specifically would cover the overhead of the business in the event I became disabled. We rely on the passive income from our investments to replace my income from the business.

LONGEVITY

Americans' increasing longevity can be an economic blessing or a curse. Provided we remain healthy, increased longevity increases our human capital. If our mental and physical health decline as we age, our human capital is diminished.

Thus, there are two other things you can do to increase your odds of financial success, and they have nothing to do with saving or investing. First, take care of your body, and second, take care of your mind. Quit smoking, eat right, and exercise. These are as much a part of achieving lasting financial success as is a sound investment strategy.

chapter 19

STAY ON TOP OF YOUR INSURANCE

We are ready for any unforeseen event that may or may not occur.
—Dan Quayle

THERE IS ONLY ONE thing worse than not having insurance when you need it: that is, thinking you have it and finding out you don't. If you scrimp on insurance and catastrophe strikes, all your hard work can quickly go up in smoke. On the other hand, too much insurance drains cash you could have put to better use elsewhere.

I have experienced this firsthand. In 1998, a fire ripped through my polo barn, killing six polo ponies and destroying the entire structure and all its contents. I had some insurance, but not nearly enough.

Originally, I had insured the building for its full replacement value. Over time, I had done some work to a small apartment in the barn and added far more stuff than I ever would have dreamed. I had no insurance on the horses.

As I went through and tried to put a price on every last item in the barn, big and small, the enormity of the financial loss dawned on me. The loss of my horses was devastating; it was like six members of my family being murdered. (Yes, the fire was ruled an arson.) But the financial loss was also stupefying.

When insuring your possessions against a total loss, I can promise you, you are probably underestimating the replacement cost. It's not the big things that will get you. You probably accounted for those. It's the hundreds, if not thousands, of little things—eight dollars here, fifteen dollars there. Pretty soon, the total is in the thousands, even tens of thousands, of dollars.

My capital loss (in other words, total loss minus insurance proceeds) was in excess of $200,000. Inexcusably, I knew I was underinsured, but I didn't do anything about it. Like everyone, I kept saying to myself, I'll get around to it someday.

Here's something else you don't know until you've experienced a loss of this magnitude. In order to get paid by the insurance company, you have to have receipts—at least I did. You might remember my earlier confession that I hate paper, and I am notorious for throwing away anything I haven't touched in the last year.

Keep a file of your important receipts and appraisals. (Obviously, you'll want to store them away from your house, where they could go up in smoke.) If possible, scan them and keep copies off-site somewhere. Failing that, periodically put paper receipts in a folder in a safe deposit box. If catastrophe strikes, it may mean the difference between getting the full insurance settlement you are entitled to and not. At a minimum, it will make your life much less stressful at a time when it already seems to be coming unraveled.

In business, when times are tough, the first things to get cut are marketing and R&D. It's human nature. But human nature is wrong. You are betting your future, and it almost always turns out to be the wrong decision.

Family CFOs often make the exact same mistake. When times are tough, insurance is one of the first things to go. A decision is made to keep the cable television but to stop paying for insurance! This is a *big* mistake! *Huge!* Insurance is a necessity. Find the cost savings in the nonessential expenditures. Walk or take the bus. I don't care what you have to do, but don't mess with your insurance. Remember the lesson on compounding. Similarly, a catastrophic loss is magnified and is extremely difficult to recover from.

On the flip side of the coin, don't insure what you can afford to lose. I once met a couple who had several million dollars in the bank. Both of their grown children had done extremely well for themselves. Yet, this couple was still paying for $2 million life insurance policies on both the husband and the wife. This was totally unnecessary. The surviving spouse would have more than enough money to live comfortably on to the end of his/her life, and the next generation didn't need the money.

Be objective. The key with insurance is to have just enough and nothing more. As part of the monthly or quarterly review of your financials, make sure you and your spouse regularly review all insurance policies and their limits. As things change, make sure you update your coverage as appropriate.

Here's one final word of warning. Make sure you understand very clearly what is and is not covered under your insurance policies. Let me share another firsthand experience. I used to live in a high-rise condo in Dallas. One May, a torrential rainfall hit the Dallas–Fort Worth area. The underground parking garage in my building went down four levels. It filled with water all the way up to the first level. Porsches, Vipers, and even a Rolls Royce sat under water in that garage. Hundreds of cars were destroyed.

Fortunately, I was out of town that weekend and had parked at the airport, so my car was spared.

Unfortunately, I was not completely off the hook. Each condo had a storage unit in the basement of the building. The only thing I had of real value in my storage unit was a set of china my mother and father had received when they got married. The flood smashed it to smithereens.

No problem. My homeowner's policy would take care of it, right? Well, that's what I thought, but I soon learned that such policies don't cover flooding. And who would have thought I needed *flood insurance* living on the fifth floor of a high-rise in uptown Dallas?

A good rule of thumb to remember is this: the cheaper the policy you get, the less it is likely to cover. Some policies are so full of exclusions and caveats they aren't worth the paper they are written on. Make sure you understand your policy, and if your insurance agent won't patiently explain it to you, get a new insurance agent.

chapter 20

TAKE CARE OF HEALTH CARE

Those who do not find time for exercise will have to find time for illness.
—Earl of Derby, British Prime Minister

EVERYTHING I SAID IN the previous chapter about life, property, and casualty insurance also applies to health insurance. Instead of fire or flood, think cancer, stroke, heart attack, or Alzheimer's. Our own human frailty has the power to wipe out a lifetime of saving. Make sure you have sufficient medical and long-term care insurance.

This is of major concern as we get older. The cost of health care, and therefore the cost of health care insurance, is rising at twice the rate of inflation.[91] Don't underestimate the need.

My dentist told me I needed two crowns. The cost was $3,500. I shattered my ankle in a horseback riding accident. The ankle had to be surgically repaired with plates and screws. The surgery and one night in the hospital, plus all the follow-up care, cost almost $10,000.

A private room in a nursing home today costs about $70,000 a year.[92] My grandmother lived more than ten years of her life in a nursing home after a debilitating stroke. That's $700,000, not including the medical care she required.

If you have enough millions in the bank to cover these kinds of costs, you can self-insure the health care risk. But the rest of us need to make sure we have adequate health care coverage including medical, dental, and—if you are over 55—long-term care insurance.

A standard of rule of thumb says you shouldn't spend more than 7.5 percent of your annual income toward long-term care insurance premiums. If the insurance costs more than that as a percentage of your income, you would be better off without it.[93]

Let's say you are a relatively healthy married 65-year-old. Ballpark, you would expect to pay an insurance premium of around $1,300 a year.[94] Of course, prices will vary a lot from state to state and from person to person, depending on the coverage, and they will certainly go up over time. But using $1,300 for illustration purposes, the income floor would be $17,333 in annual income ($1,300 ÷ .075). If your income was $17,333 or less, you should not purchase long-term care insurance.

There is also a point, on the upside, at which long-term care insurance becomes unnecessary. If you have between $3 and $5 million in assets, you can afford to skip long-term care insurance,[95] because you can afford to pay out of pocket any expenses you might incur. (I know! I know! If you had $3 million you wouldn't be reading this book. Still, when you become a multimillionaire, you'll know.) It is the person who falls in between those two thresholds who needs long-term care insurance.

Almost everyone these days understands the value of healthcare insurance. I talk with people every day who have enough passive income to retire but don't because they don't want to lose their health care benefits. But only 7 million people in the United States have long-term care insurance.[96] Maybe it is because the product is fairly new, and to be fair, it does have some problems.

A March 26, 2007, report in the *New York Times* suggested that after years of paying premiums, many long-term care policyholders had their claims systematically denied by insurers.[97] There's also the possibility that an insurance company may raise your premiums down the road. To some extent, I think people approach long-term care insurance a lot like they do a will. They are resistant because they don't want to think about a circumstance in which they can no longer care for themselves.

Nonetheless, both health care and long-term care insurance serve important roles in managing risk for the family CFO. If you don't have this coverage and you need either or both, get the coverage appropriate for you.

chapter 21

PROTECT YOUR
IDENTITY

Americans may have no identity,
but they do have wonderful teeth.
— Jean Baudrillard

IDENTITY THEFT IS A real concern for consumers: more than 217 million people have been affected by data breaches since 2005.[98] According to a study by Gartner, Inc., research analysts and consultants, 15 million people were victimized by identity theft in 2005 alone. That is the equivalent of one person every two seconds.[99]

Most of these identity theft cases go unsolved. Financial institutions eat the costs and then pass them on to consumers. That makes identity theft costly in terms of time, money, and stress.

Victims report spending an average of 330 hours over a period of four to six months trying to straighten out the effects of identity theft.[100] Even after the identity thief stops using your stolen data, victims suffer as a result. Aftereffects include "increased cost of insurance or credit card fees, inability to find a job, higher interest rates and battling collection agencies and issuers who refuse to clear records despite substantiating evidence of the crime. This 'tail' may continue for more than ten years after the crime was first discovered."[101]

So clearly, being aware of all the different forms of identity theft is important for the family CFO. It is equally important that you know what will and won't protect you from identity theft.

If you think identity theft involves just credit cards, you are badly underestimating the risk. Identity theft can take many forms. The definition of identity theft is someone wrongfully using your personal information to obtain credit, loans, services, even rentals and mortgages in your name. Imagine the nightmare if someone commits a crime while using your identity!

I know a baseball star who wouldn't report the theft of his wife's credit cards because the thief spends less than she does.

—Joe Garagiola

So, what should you do to protect yourself and your family from identity theft? The Federal Trade Commission breaks down the strategy into the easy-to-remember slogan, "Deter. Detect. Defend." I prefer to work on deterring and detecting so that I won't have to do a lot of work defending—that is, cleaning up the mess.

DETER

Here are a handful of the best tips for deterring identity theft, culled from the Internet.

- Buy a crosscut shredder and use it to shred anything with identifying information or account numbers on it that you throw away.

This would include credit card receipts, preapproved credit card offers, insurance forms, physician statements, checks and bank statements, and expired credit cards. Do not throw anything in the garbage that could be used to piece together your identity.

- Opt for paperless statements from your vendors. Banks, utilities, brokerage firms, retailers, and credit card companies all save money when they don't have to mail you a bill or statement. Less paper means less risk of identity theft.

- Protect your Social Security number. Don't carry your Social Security card in your wallet. Don't write or print it on your checks. If someone uses your Social Security number as an account number, ask them to change it to something else. Many companies that ask for your Social Security number will accept two forms of identification as a substitute. Don't assume that just because someone asks for it, you have to give it out.

- Don't put checks in the mail from your home mailbox. Mail theft is common. Drop them off at the post office or a post office drop box.

- Remove mail from your mailbox promptly. Don't let it sit there waiting for a thief to lift it. If you are going to be on vacation, be sure someone will pick up your mail each day while you are gone, or go to usps.gov to put a vacation hold on your mail.

- When you request a new credit card, put a note in your tickler file. If it doesn't arrive promptly, call the credit card issuer and find out if it was returned. If it wasn't returned, be sure to ask if someone has filed a change-of-address request. That someone is an identity thief.

- Never give out personal information over the phone, by mail, or over the Internet unless you initiated the contact. Identity thieves are constantly becoming more and more sophisticated. Posing as a representative of a legitimate business is standard operating procedure. Call them back at a known number or search for the URL rather than clicking on a link in an e-mail.

- Keep your personal information in a secure place at home and at work. Forty-three percent of identity theft victims said they knew the imposter.[102] Don't underestimate the possibility that a housekeeper, babysitter, or outside contractor could heist your sensitive information.

- Create "strong" passwords. These are passwords that include letters, numbers, and special characters as well as upper- and lowercase. For a list of great ideas on how to build strong passwords, visit www.lifehack.org.

- Don't use the same password for every site, and don't write them down on a piece of paper or in a spreadsheet. Plenty of password managers are available these days, and many of them are free. An Internet search for "password manager" will turn up loads of options. One of the best is RoboForm. If you are mobile like me, or want to share your password file with your spouse, try Pass-Pack. Jim and I have started using it recently and I think it is outstanding.

- Make sure your firewall and wireless systems are secured. I am still amazed at how many homes and businesses have unsecured wireless networks. If you have a laptop or wireless device permanently attached to your hand like I do, you know you can find an unsecured access point to "borrow" in almost any building or neighborhood.

- Do not store credit card numbers, passwords, or any other sensitive information on laptops, PDAs, or SmartPhones.

- Do not expose sensitive information while using public networks like hotels, cafes, airports, or libraries. Be wary of connections named "free public wifi." Ask the store or hotel for the name of their network. The big companies that advertise their wireless connection tend to be pretty safe. But be aware, someone sitting next to you can easily set up a network with the same name. Bottom line: Use common sense and you will probably be OK.

DETECT

Early detection is the key to minimizing damage to your credit and the time required to clean it up. Take these steps on a regular basis to make sure you detect identity theft.

- Do not just throw your statements in a drawer. Check all statements carefully for anything that looks out of place or you can't identify.
- Check your credit reports at least once a year. Look for accounts you didn't open and debts you didn't incur. You are entitled to a free credit report from each of the three major credit reporting agencies once a year. To get yours, go to www.annualcreditreport.com.

SHOULD I PAY FOR SERVICES THAT SUPPOSEDLY PROTECT MY IDENTITY?

A number of services are available nowadays to help deter and detect identity theft. Many companies offer to put a freeze on your credit file. Others provide credit-monitoring services. Are they worth it?

I think they are. It's a trade-off, though. You have to understand exactly what you are paying for and what these companies can help you with and what they cannot.

Jim and I use a company called LifeLock. LifeLock puts a fraud alert on your credit file and resets it every 90 days.

I bought Jim a new HD flat-screen television for his birthday. When Dish Network tried to open an account in our name, a representative from Dish Network called us and asked a long series of questions to ensure that we really were who we said we were. It worked like a charm.

LifeLock also automatically requests our free credit reports for us each year. They request that your name be taken off all preapproved credit card and junk mail lists. If we ever lose a wallet or purse, they help contact all the credit card companies, banks, and other document issuers to close accounts, get new credit cards, and have driver's licenses and other documents reissued.

Finally, if our identity ever is stolen, they promise to do whatever it takes to restore our good name, up to $1,000,000 in expenses. Will they really do all these things? I hope I never find out. But if nothing else, I know that they set the fraud alerts, my junk mail has been greatly reduced, and my credit reports do appear once a year.

You can get more money, but you cannot get more time.

—Jim Rohn

Could I do all of these things myself? Absolutely. But for me, it is a question of (1) how likely am I to remember to do them? and (2) how much is my time worth? For about a hundred bucks per person, per year, to me it's worth it.

Is it the be-all and end-all of identity theft protection? No. I still have to do all the other things I listed. LifeLock only protects me from someone opening a new credit file in my name. It does nothing to protect me from the unauthorized use of existing accounts or things like phishing scams. But still, some protection is better than none in my book.

Many independent companies, credit card companies, and even the credit reporting agencies themselves offer credit-monitoring services. We used to get this service through CitiBank, and I thought it was quite good. We could pull up all three of our credit reports at any time. CitiBank also alerted us if anything material changed. We could see the various accounts, the reported balances, and our credit scores for each reporting agency.

Personally, I think once a year is too long to go between credit report checks. In this day and age, your credit is one of your most important assets. It needs to be managed like your other assets, and timely information is crucial if the family CFO is going to manage effectively. The question you have to ask yourself is, "What is each family member's identity worth, and how much time or money am I willing to spend to protect each person's identity?"

There was a time no identity thief would have wanted my credit. Any company would have laughed at him/her when he/she tried to open a new account. In fact, they would have probably hit the identity thief up for some of my past due payments! But I worked really long and hard to get a pristine credit report. Now, it's worth a lot to me to protect it.

MEDICAL IDENTITY THEFT

One last note about a really scary form of identity theft. Not only can this theft cost you time, money, and aggravation, it can potentially kill you! I'm talking about medical identity theft.

Medical identity theft occurs when someone uses your information, such as a health insurance identification or Social Security number, to get healthcare or to obtain reimbursement from insurers and others for false claims. When this happens, it is quite possible your medical history and healthcare records can include someone else's information. Under certain situations, this can be life threatening. Imagine you are in an accident, for example, and they transfuse you with the wrong blood type.

Unfortunately, there is little you can do to protect yourself from medical identity theft beyond the measures already noted above. Most medical identity theft occurs when insiders at doctor's offices and hospitals steal and sell medical records in bulk. This is a lucrative market in which a medical file goes for as much as $50 on the street.[103]

Still, it pays to be aware of the problem so you can spot it if it happens to you.

chapter 22

MANAGE YOUR CREDIT SCORE

Don't it always seem to go
That you don't know what you've got
'Til it's gone.
They paved paradise
And put up a parking lot.
—Joni Mitchell

ACCORDING TO THE EXPERIAN National Score Index™, the average credit score in America is 692. Approximately 58 percent of Americans have credit scores above 700. Only 13 percent have scores above 800. At the other extreme, 15 percent of Americans have scores below 550.[104] Experts typically call anything in the 700s a "good" score.

Do you know your score? I never understood the value of good credit until mine was wrecked. I don't know what my credit score was at its lowest point, but I know it was appalling. Late payments, bills sent to collections, repossessions, and charge-offs make for a pretty ugly credit report.

What I learned the hard way was the extent to which your credit score can determine where you live, what job you get, and how much you pay for the things you need. I now view my credit rating as an important asset that I guard very carefully.

Understanding and managing your credit is even more critical in today's credit economy, where good credit is both increasingly valuable and increasingly difficult to achieve. To be a good family CFO, you have to know your credit score, understand the credit scoring process, and—when necessary—take advantage of tools that can help you improve your credit.

WHAT YOU NEED TO KNOW ABOUT CREDIT SCORING

Credit scores are a numerical representation of your credit history at a given point in time. Your credit score is a number used by lenders as an indication of how likely you are to repay your obligations. Credit scores are generated by a credit scoring model that uses the data from your credit report.

Your credit report will contain a fairly up-to-date credit history plus such additional information as address history, marital status, employment history, and other details that may help creditors judge your creditworthiness.

Your credit history includes balances, credit limits, and payment history for all accounts past and present, joint and individual, as well as any credit applications, judgments, bankruptcies, and tax liens.

There are three big credit bureaus. Each credit bureau's report may contain slightly different information. Often this is caused by differences in what information the bureaus receive from creditors and when they receive it. You should be aware that "25 percent of all consumer credit reports may contain errors that can result in the denial of access to credit," according to a report by the Federal Reserve.[105]

And, as if this were not challenging enough, the elements of credit scoring change over time, much like Google's search algorithms, which creates myths and misinformation. So, here is what you need to know in order to manage your credit score effectively.

- Credit scores change every time new data are reported to a credit bureau. Every time new data are added or information is removed, your score can and will change.
- Payment history is key. A history of paying on time proves your creditworthiness more than anything else. Late payments or missed payments will have an immediate negative effect, even if this occurs just once.
- Keeping balances below 50 percent of the available credit or loan amount on each account will generally improve your credit score. On the flip side, going over credit limits and consistently using all available credit are going to lower your score.
- Using credit to make purchases and then making on-time payments—or, even better, consistently paying off the balance—demonstrates financial responsibility. If you never use credit, there are no good data by which to judge your ability to manage credit.
- The longer your credit history, the better. How long an account has been open, the average age of all accounts, and when accounts were last used all factor into credit scores.
- Identify and fix errors or omissions. We already talked about the number of reports that have errors. If one of your credit reports is missing information or contains incorrect information, get it fixed.

CREDIT MANAGEMENT TOOLS
FOR THE FAMILY CFO

Maybe you have heard the terms *credit repair*, *credit restoration*, and *credit optimization*. If you are like most people, you are probably unsure what the difference is among these terms, whether these services can help, or whether these services are just a scam.

All of these terms, as commonly used in late-night television advertising, refer to the same thing. The companies that offer these services promise to improve your credit score by cleaning up your credit report—for a fee, of course. The fees can range from a few hundred to a few thousand dollars.

We are right to cast a wary eye toward these credit repair/restoration/optimization companies. Let's face it. If we really have late payments, collections, bankruptcies, and charge-offs, anything these companies do must be somewhat shady, right? That is, if they do anything at all.

Some credit repair companies legitimately help you deal with erroneous items on your credit report. But for most of these types of companies, that service is just a front. Many employ tactics such as file segregation, piggybacking, and bulk disputing of negative items with credit bureaus. Some even offer to invent a "new" credit identity—and then, a new credit report—by applying for an employer identification number to use instead of your Social Security number. Technically, these tactics fall on a spectrum ranging from questionable to illegal. All of them are trying to remove or conceal a legitimate boo-boo from your credit file. I'll talk more about that in a minute.

Credit simulation is different from credit repair. Credit simulation uses technology to determine, in advance, the effect of various actions on your credit score. For example, what will happen to my credit score if I am 30 days late on a single payment, or apply for a department store credit card, or take out a mortgage?

The company that developed and computes your credit score is Fair Isaac. They have a number of services through myfico.com that include their credit score simulator. Others offer similar products, but I prefer to go straight to the source. The Fair Isaac simulator uses your actual credit score as a starting point. Others use an estimate based on a series of questions.

These simulations can be useful in managing your credit score. Is it better to leave an account open with a zero balance or close it completely? Which accounts should I close? Which card should I pay down to have the biggest impact? What items are creating the biggest drag on my score?

I have used both a credit repair agency and simulators in the past to help manage my score. Almost seven years ago, when Jim and I consolidated households, I had a problem with my cable bill. When I called them to disconnect my cable because I was moving, they told me a credit would be issued to my account. Instead of paying the bill they had just sent me, I decided to wait, assuming they would be sending me a revised bill reflecting the credit.

They did, but not until the next billing cycle. Keep in mind that I had, by that point, gone years paying all of my bills on time and waiting for all those old scars to drop off my credit report. Even though I had paid every bill with the cable company on time up to that point, I missed a single payment—I was waiting for their adjusted bill—and they sent it to collections! I couldn't believe it.

I had worked so hard to keep my credit perfect, I don't mind telling you I was pissed! To add insult to injury, I remember the amount of the adjusted bill was a piddly ten dollars or less.

I called and pleaded my case with the cable company, the collection agency, and the credit bureau. No one would budge. I had missed a payment. The company had a policy of sending missed payments directly to collections when the account was closed. No one would remove the blemish from my credit report even though I had paid the bill as soon as the corrected one arrived.

As a last resort, I called a local credit repair company. I paid them a ridiculous amount of money to remove that collection from my credit report. I didn't care what it cost. It was the principle.

Here's how that credit repair worked. There are two federal laws dealing with credit reporting: the Fair Credit Reporting Act (FCRA) and the Fair and Accurate Credit Transactions Act (FACTA). Those laws are meant to guarantee consumers that only fair, accurate, and verifiable information appears on their credit report. *Verifiable* is the key word.

You have the right to dispute the veracity of any item on your report. When you do, the credit bureau contacts the creditor and asks them to verify the item in question. If they do not respond within 30 days, the credit bureau must remove the item. Here is where it starts to get into a gray area for some.

The credit repair agency automates this process and continually disputes the item until the creditor fails to respond. I can only imagine this happens fairly regularly. I suspect the older the item, the more likely it is to get dropped. What company wants to spend payroll dollars on clerks verifying old bills that have long since been paid or written off? It's just not a good use of their personnel.

So, long story short, my issue disappeared from my credit report in only a month or two. Could I have done it myself for a lot less money? Probably. But again, what is my time worth? Was it a legitimate item on my credit? Technically, yes. Do I feel bad about having them repair a legitimate item? Not one bit. Would I do it again? Absolutely.

There's a footnote to the story. Several years later I got a letter from the Federal Trade Commission or some similar agency. Apparently, the company I had used was being investigated for fraudulent advertising.

I guess they were looking for people to say the company had ripped them off.

As far as I was concerned, they did exactly what they promised they would do. The fee was excessive, but they told me what it was up front, and to me it was worth it. I had no complaints. I never responded to the government inquiry.

chapter 23

GET STARTED

A body in motion stays in motion. A body at rest stays at rest.
—Newton's First Law of Motion (paraphrased)

SO, THIS IS WHERE the rubber meets the road! It's time to get serious about being the family CFO.

By now you should have a pretty good idea of what to do in each of the four key areas: plan prudently, save prodigiously, invest wisely, and manage risk.

You've read this far, so clearly you are motivated by financial success. So what next? How do you take the ideas in this book and put them into action?

While it is possible to take the chapters in any order and start working the key points, I strongly recommend you start with the end in mind.

That means starting with a vision, a plan for achieving the vision, and a set of personal financial statements. Once you have those three items firmly in hand, then you can attack the rest of the action items in any order you choose.

So get started, and let me know how it goes. I would love to hear how you have put the ideas in this book to work for you and your family. You can reach me by e-mail at ksnider@snideradvisors.com.

AFTERWORD

No one saves us but ourselves. No one can and no one may.
We ourselves must walk the path.
—Buddha

THERE ARE ONLY THREE ways to become rich: inherit it, marry it, or earn it. Most of us aren't heirs to a fortune, and unless your parents are in the minority, they are going to need all they have just to live out their power years. Some of us may be fortunate enough to marry into wealth, but I certainly wouldn't recommend it as a wealth-building strategy. It reminds me of the line in the movie *Pretty Woman*: "Meet the Olson sisters. They have made marrying well an art form."

So that leaves earning it. The good news is that the road to financial success is well traveled, and those who have gone before you have left it pretty well marked. The only thing required from you is the discipline to make it happen.

The next step is up to you. My hope for you is that you pick up the mantle of family CFO and run with it. It is arguably the most important job you will ever hold.

APPENDIX: GENERAL DISCLAIMERS

Snider Advisors makes no representation that the information and opinions expressed in this book are accurate, complete, or current. The opinions expressed should not be construed as financial, legal, tax, or other advice and are provided for informational purposes only. All investments involve risk, including possible loss of principal.

SNIDER INVESTMENT METHOD®

The Snider Investment Method is a long-term strategy designed to create portfolio income. It uses a combination of stock, options, and cash, along with specific techniques applied in a specific sequence, to achieve these goals. We teach the proprietary Snider Investment Method, a sensible, step-by-step approach to investing designed for the do-it-yourself investor. Investment objectives, risks, and other information are contained in the Snider Investment Method Owner's Manual; read and consider them carefully before investing. All investments, including the Snider Investment Method, are subject to risk, including possible loss of principal.

HISTORICAL PERFORMANCE OF THE SNIDER INVESTMENT METHOD®

The yields quoted in this book are based on the accounts managed by Snider Advisors, beginning in September 2002, through February 2008. The average annualized yield for the entire sample was 13.3 percent after transaction costs.

Investors in accounts that can borrow on margin had annualized yields 4.5 percent higher than those in accounts without margin (such as IRAs). The average for margin accounts was 15.6 percent and the average for non-margin accounts was 11.1 percent. Smaller accounts had annualized yields about 1.2 percent lower than the retirement-size accounts (over $250,000). All terminated accounts are included up to the last completed month. The annualized yield for each month in each account is weighted equally in calculating the average.

CALCULATION OF YIELDS

The yield calculation is different than the return calculation shown by most in the investment industry. The percentage yield is the yield for the month divided by the stake. The stake is all contributions minus withdrawals, plus the profits from any closed positions. The yield is then multiplied by 12 to get an annualized rate.

Note that some months are actually four weeks and some are five weeks, and the first month of an account can be shorter or longer. No adjustment is made for these differences, which are expected to be minor.

These yields are shown for illustrative purposes only. These are not a guarantee of yields an investor would receive by investing using the Snider Investment Method®.

FACTORS THAT CAN AFFECT YIELDS

The yields quoted were obtained by using methods substantially similar to those taught in the Snider Method workshop. The yields of any one individual investor can be greater than or less than the average, and the average of future periods can be greater than or less than the average of past periods.

The Snider Investment Method focuses on stocks that pass well-defined bankruptcy screening tests based on academic research. Within these stocks, the Snider Investment Method selects those with a liquid option market and high option premiums.

The objective is to select stocks of companies with a low probability of bankruptcy but higher than average price volatility. The yields are primarily due to option premiums. These premiums are higher when interest rates and the anticipated future volatility of stock prices are high. Both these factors have been low by historical standards over the time period measured, but they could be higher or lower in the future.

POSSIBILITY OF LOSSES

Investors who terminate positions prematurely can experience realized losses, sometimes greater than the yield realized over the lifetime of the position. For this reason, investors should be able to leave the principal invested (or reinvested after a position closes) for a minimum of two years. Some positions may not close within two years.

Finally, the Snider Investment Method® does involve investment in stocks. If a company were to declare bankruptcy, there would be a permanent loss of the capital invested. There have been no bankruptcies in the period covered, but that does not mean the chances of bankruptcy are zero.

REGARDING DISCUSSED RESULTS

The results quoted in this document are averages. Some investors do better than the average and some do worse. Results are also past performance, and past performance is not indicative of future results.

REGARDING OPTIONSXPRESS

Snider Advisors has an economic incentive to recommend options Xpress. Specifically, as part of a loan agreement with optionsXpress, Snider Advisors receives payment in the form of a loan reduction for each new account it refers to optionsXpress and any of its affiliates. More detailed information about the loan agreement and our fiduciary responsibility can be found in ADVII (Schedule F). Please contact Snider Advisors with any questions regarding its relationship with optionsXpress and the terms of the agreement with optionsXpress.

RESOURCES

Books

Bach, David. *The Automatic Millionaire: A Powerful One-Step Plan to Live and Finish Rich.* 1st ed. (New York: Broadway Books, 2004).

Ramsey, Dave. *Financial Peace* (New York: Viking, 1997).

Stanley, Thomas J. *The Millionaire Next Door: The Surprising Secrets of America's Wealthy* (Atlanta: Longstreet Press, 1996).

For a complete list of the books I recommend for family CFOs, see my Recommended Reading List at snideradvisors.com or howto-bethefamilycfo.com.

Estate Tax Calculators

"Estate Tax Calculator," *banksite.com* <http://www.banksite.com/calc/estate> [accessed 15 March 2008].

"Estate Tax Planning—Financial Calculators from Dinkytown.net," *Financial Calculators from Dinkytown.net* <http://www.dinkytown.net/java/EstatePlan.html> [accessed 15 March 2008].

Financial Services Firms Used by the Author

ING Direct, Orange Savings Account, www.ingdirect.com

optionsXpress,* online brokerage firm, www.optionsxpress.com

Organizations

National Association of Personal Financial Planners (NAPFA), www.napfa.org

Software

Microsoft Money (www.microsoft.com/money)

PassPack (www.passpack.com)

Quicken (quicken.intuit.com)

RoboForm (www.roboform.com)

Web Sites

How to Be the Family CFO book site (www.howtobethefamilycfo.com)

LifeHack (www.lifehack.org)

---

*See the appendix for disclosures regarding optionsXpress.

Author's Contact Information

Kim Snider
Snider Advisors
ksnider@snideradvisors.com
Direct: 214-245-5236
Toll-Free: 888-SNIDER-7
www.snideradvisors.com

NOTES

Introduction

1. Annamaria Lusardi and Olivia S. Mitchell, *SSRN–Financial Literacy and Retirement Preparedness: Evidence and Implications for Financial Education Programs* (Michigan Retirement Research Center, 2007), <http://ssrn.com/abstract=957796> [accessed 15 April 2008].

2. Danna Moore, *Survey of Financial Literacy in Washington State: Knowledge, Behavior, Attitudes, and Experiences* (Pullman, WA: Social and Economic Sciences Research Center, Washington State University, 2003), <http://www.dfi.wa.gov/news/finlitsurvey.pdf> [accessed 15 April 2008].

3. Flore-Ann Messy, "Challenges of Financial Education in the Insurance Sector," September 2006, <http://www.oecd.org/dataoecd/15/48/37424761.pdf> [accessed 15 April 2008].

4. Scott Hodge and J. Scott Moody, *Wealthy Americans and Business Activity* (Washington, D.C.: The Tax Foundation, 2004), <http://www.taxfoundation.org/files/1d68c0e2054ad7e51ec0a90b9d989e5f.pdf> [accessed 2 March 2008].

5. "2003 GEM Report Finds Uptick in U.S. Entrepreneurial Activity," *Babson College*, 8 January 2004, <http://www3.babson.edu/Newsroom/Releases/IntlGEM2003.cfm> [accessed 2 March 2008].

6. "Dream on: Many Americans say middle class faces impossible savings task," *MarketWatch.com*, 21 March 2007, <http://www.marketwatch.com/News/Story/many-americans-say-middle-class/story.aspx?guid=%7bB6CCFB9E-6179-4C0C-9909-E10AC69308E9%7d&print=true&dist=printTop> [accessed 2 March 2008].

Chapter 1—What Is a Family CFO?

7.   ICI Research Staff, *2007 Investment Company Fact Book* (Washington, D.C.: Investment Company Institute, 2007), <http://www.icifactbook. org/pdf/2007_factbook.pdf> [accessed 3 March 2008].

Chapter 2—Why Should I Become a Capable Family CFO?

8.   Paul Schott Stevens, "Mutual Fund Investing: The Power and Promise of a Simple Idea," 2 August 2006, <http://www.ici.org/issues/fserv/ 06_aust_stevens_remarks.html> [accessed 3 March 2008].

9.   "U.S. Tax Code On-Line," *Fourmilab.ca,* <http://www.fourmilab.ch/uscode/26usc/> [accessed 24 July 2007].

10.   Richard W. Johnson, Gordon B. T. Mermin, and Cori E. Uccello, *When the Nest Egg Cracks: Financial Consequences of Health Problems, Marital Status Changes and Job Layoffs at Older Ages* (Chestnut Hill, MA: Center for Retirement Research at Boston College, 2005), <http://www.bc.edu/centers/crr/ papers/WP_2005-18.pdf> [accessed 3 March 2008].

11.   Jack VanDerhei, *Retirement Income Adequacy After PPA and FAS 158: Part One—Plan Sponsors' Reactions Issue Brief* (Washington, D.C.: Employee Benefit Research Institute, 2007), <http://www.ebri.org/pdf/briefspdf/EBRI_ IB_07-20079.pdf> [accessed 3 March 2008].

Chapter 4—Have a Plan, but Don't Overplan

12.   Dan Poynter, *Dan Poynter's Self-Publishing Manual: How to Write, Print and Sell Your Own Book,* 16th ed., completely rev. (Santa Barbara, CA: Para Pub, 2007).

13.   Kraig Kramers, "Vistage Podcast: The Professional CEO's Toolkit" [accessed 2 March 2007].

Chapter 5—Plan Now for the Inevitable

14.   Constance J. Fontaine, "The basics of estate planning (page 3 of 4)," *Bankrate.com,* <http://www.bankrate.com/brm/news/ retirementguide2007/20070501_estate_planning_a3.asp?caret=3f> [accessed 9 March 2008].

15. Butch Knowlton, "The Gist of It Is This," *Virginia's Lodge*, <http://www.virginiaslodge.com/htms/vallecito/mrf.htm> [accessed 14 March 2008].

16. "Checklist: Reasons to Update Your Will & Estate Planning Documents," *FindLaw*, <http://estate.findlaw.com/estate-planning/estate-planning-forms/le20_g.html> [accessed 15 March 2008].

Chapter 6—Create a Six-Month Emergency Fund

17. Johnson, et al., ibid.

Chapter 7—Know the Difference Between Good Debt and Bad Debt

18. "U.S. bankruptcies soared 38 percent in 2007: government," Yahoo News, 15 April 2008, <http://news.yahoo.com/s/nm/20080415/us_nm/usa_economy_bankruptcies_dc> [accessed 20 April 2008].

19. "Credit Card Statistics," *CardRatings*, <http://www.cardratings.com/creditcardstatistics.html> [accessed 20 April 2008].

20. "History of credit cards," *Did You Know?* <http://www.didyouknow.cd/creditcards.htm> [accessed 20 April 2008].

21. Paul Bannister, "Bankrate's Guide to Consolidating Your Debt: 25 fascinating facts about debt," *Bankrate.com*, 20 September 2004, <http://www.bankrate.com/brm/news/debt/debtguide2004/debt-trivia1.asp> [accessed 19 April 2008].

22. Theresa Howard, "Advertisers forced to think way outside the box," *USA Today*, 19 June 2005, <http://www.usatoday.com/money/advertising/adtrack/2005-06-19-cannes-box_x.htm> [accessed 20 April 2008].

23. Ben Woolsey, "Credit card industry facts and personal debt statistics (2006–2007)," *CreditCards.com*, <http://www.creditcards.com/statistics/credit-card-industry-facts-and-personal-debt-statistics.php> [accessed 20 April 2008].

24. Ibid.

25. Bannister, ibid.

26. Ibid.

27. Woolsey, ibid.

28. Ibid.

29. *Recent Changes in U.S. Family Finances: Evidence from the 2001 and 2004 Survey of Consumer Finances* (Washington, D.C.: U.S. Federal Reserve Board, 2006), <http://www.federalreserve.gov/pubs/bulletin/2006/financesurvey.pdf> [accessed 20 April 2008].

30. Andrea Coombes, "Average credit card interest rates fall to two-year low: Survey," *MarketWatch.com*, 13 March 2008, <http://www.marketwatch.com/news/story/average-credit-card-interest-rates/story.aspx?guid=%7BC443BA90-1984-4E3E-B0A3-0F762DCEBF74%7D> [accessed 20 April 2008].

31. Credit Card Statistics.

32. Bannister, ibid.

33. Ibid.

34. Ibid.

35. Ibid.

36. Ibid.

37. Mary Hopkins, "Survey: Grad students' credit card debt averages $8,216," *CreditCards.com*, 4 October 2007, <http://www.creditcards.com/graduate-student-credit-card-debt.php> [accessed 20 April 2008].

38. Personal Saving Rate (Washington, D.C.: Bureau of Economic Analysis, 2008), <http://www.bea.gov/briefrm/saving.htm> [accessed 21 April 2008].

39. Bannister, ibid.

40. Gene Amromin, Jennifer Huang, and Clemens Sialm, *The Tradeoff Between Mortgage Prepayment and Tax-Deferred Retirement Savings* (Chicago: Federal Reserve Bank of Chicago, 2006), <http://www.chicagofed.org/publications/workingpapers/wp2006_05.pdf> [accessed 19 April 2008].

41. Ibid.

Chapter 8—Take Full Advantage of Tax-Deferred Retirement Accounts

42. "401k Hardship Withdrawals—An Overview," *401k Help Center*, <http://www.401khelpcenter.com/hardships.html> [accessed 19 April 2008].

43. Ibid.

44. "When Is a 401k Distribution Not Subject to the 10% Penalty?" *401k Help Center,* <http://www.401khelpcenter.com/401k_education/tenpercent.html> [accessed 19 April 2008].

45. "401k Plan Loans —An Overview," *401k Help Center,* <http://www.401khelpcenter.com/loans.html> [accessed 19 April 2008].

Chapter 9 — Save for Retirement First, then Your Kids' College

46. "America's Best Colleges 2008: Southern Methodist University," *U.S. News & World Report,* <http://colleges.usnews.rankingsandreviews.com/usnews/edu/college/directory/brief/drglance_3613_brief.php> [accessed 19 April 2008].

47. "America's Best Colleges 2008: University of Colorado–Boulder," *U.S. News & World Report,* <http://colleges.usnews.rankingsandreviews.com/usnews/edu/college/directory/brief/drglance_1370_brief.php> [accessed 19 April 2008].

48. "Press Release— U.S. Workers Save More, Are Better Prepared for Retirement but Retire Later Than Most, According to Global AXA Survey; Americans See 55 as 'Ideal' Retirement Age," *AXA Group,* 19 January 2005, <http://www.axaonline.com/rs/axa/pressroom/2005/01192005_AXA_retirement_scope.html> [accessed 20 April 2008].

49. Sandra Block, "Put retirement savings first before college fund," *USA Today,* 19 March 2006, <http://usatoday.printthis.clickability.com/pt/cpt?action=cpt&title=USATODAY.com+-+Put+retirement+savings+first+before+college+fund&expire=&urlID=14218184&fb=Y&url=http%3A%2F%2Fwww.usatoday.com%2Fmoney%2Fperfi%2Fretirement%2F2005-05-12-mym-retire_x.htm&partnerID=1661> [accessed 19 April 2008].

Chapter 11 — Know Your Strengths and Weaknesses

50. Adam Levy, "Money drives us crazy: It's official," *The Australian,* 9 February 2006.

51. Paul Slovic, "Psychological Study of Human Judgment: Implications for Investment Decision Making," *Journal of Finance* 27, no. 4 (1972).

52. Mark T. Finn and Jonathan Finn, "A Look in the Mirror," *John Mauldin's Outside the Box*, 15 January 2007, <http://www.investorsinsight.com/blogs/john_mauldins_outside_the_box/archive/2007/01/15/a-look-in-the-mirror.aspx> [accessed 20 April 2008].

Chapter 12—Start Early—Slow and Steady Wins the Race

53. *How Advisors Help Protect Investment Returns*, 2007, Quantitative Analysis of Investor Behavior (Boston, MA: Dalbar, Inc., 2007), <http://www.qaib.com/showresource.aspx?URI=howadvisorsprotectfree&Type=FreeLook> [accessed 19 April 2008].

54. *Act Now and Save* 2007, Quantitative Analysis of Investor Behavior (Boston, MA: Dalbar, Inc., 2007), <http://www.qaib.com/showresource.aspx?URI=actnowfree&Type=FreeLook> [accessed 19 April 2008].

55. Ibid.

56. Yuni Park (Media Relations Specialist, Lipper, Inc.), "Average Return U.S. Equity Mutual Funds 20 Year Rolling Period Ending 2006," 21 April 2008.

57. *Act Now and Save*, ibid.

Chapter 13—Invest Your Own Money

58. Daniel Bergstresser, John M. R. Chalmers, and Peter Tufano, "SSRN—Assessing the Costs and Benefits of Brokers in the Mutual Fund Industry," 1 October 2007, <http://ssrn.com/abstract=616981> [accessed 19 April 2008].

59. Ibid.

60. "Mutual Fund Study: Huge 'Broker Penalty' Sees Unwary Index Fund Investor Paying 3 Times More in Fund Expenses," *Zero Alpha Group*, 30 November 2006, <http://www.zeroalphagroup.com/news/113006_release.cfm> [accessed 19 April 2008].

61. Bergstresser, et al., ibid.

62. Ibid.

63. Ibid.

64. Ibid.

65. Ibid.

66. Kathy Chu, "Wall Street Snubs Small Accounts," *Wall Street Journal*, 17 February 2005, p. D2.

67. Ibid.

68. Jane Bryant Quinn, *Making the Most of Your Money*, 2nd ed. (New York: Simon & Schuster, 1997).

Chapter 14—Create Passive Income

69. James K. Glassman, *Can Americans Handle Their Own Retirement Investing Choices?* (Washington, D.C.: American Enterprise Institute for Public Policy Research, 1998), <http://www.aei.org/publications/pubID.15543,filter. all/pub_detail.asp> [accessed 20 April 2008].

70. *Act Now and Save*, ibid.

71. Lipper, Inc.

72. *Act Now and Save*, ibid.

73. Robin Goldwyn Blumenthal, "Income to spare: Where to find attractive yields for retirement," *Barron's Newsweekly*, 21 March 2005, pp. 24, 26, 28.

74. "Market Data Center: P/Es & Yields on Major Indexes," *Wall Street Journal*, 1 February 2008, <http://online.wsj.com/mdc/public/page/2_3021-peyield. html?mod=mdc_h_usshl> [accessed 1 February 2008].

75. Blumenthal, ibid.

76. "Market Data Center: ETF Snapshot for First Trust Value Line Dividend Index Fund ETF," *Wall Street Journal*, 1 February 2008, <http://online.wsj. com/public/quotes/etf_snapshot.html?&symb=FVD&sid=2562488> [accessed 1 February 2008].

77. "Fidelity Equity-Income Fund (FEQIX)," *Fidelity*, 1 February 2008, <http://personal.fidelity.com/products/funds/mfl_frame.shtml?316138106> [accessed 1 February 2008].

78. "Markets Data Center: Bond Yields," *Wall Street Journal*, 1 February 2008, <http://online.wsj.com/mdc/public/page/2_3021-bondyield. html?mod=mdc_bnd_pglnk> [accessed 1 February 2008].

79. "Emerging Market Bonds," *Morningstar*, 1 February 2008, <http://news.morningstar.com/fundReturns/FundReturns.html?category=$FOCA$EB> [accessed 1 February 2008].

80. "Market Data Center: ETF Snapshot for DJ Wilshire REIT," *Wall Street Journal*, 1 February 2008, <http://online.wsj.com/public/quotes/etf_snapshot.html?&symb=RWR&sid=2814472> [accessed 1 February 2008].

81. "Markets Data Center Home—Consumer Money Rates," *Wall Street Journal*, 1 February 2008, <http://online.wsj.com/mdc/page/marketsdata.html?mod=topnav_0_0002> [accessed 1 February 2008].

82. "Canadian Royalty Trusts Listed on U.S. Stock Exchanges," *The Dividend Detective*, 1 February 2008, <http://www.dividenddetective.com/canadian_royalty_trusts.htm> [accessed 1 February 2008].

83. "Markets Data Center: Treasury Inflation-Protected Securities (TIPS)," *Wall Street Journal*, 1 February 2008, <http://online.wsj.com/mdc/public/page/2_3020-tips.html?mod=mdc_bnd_pglnk> [accessed 1 February 2008].

Chapter 15—Control What You Can; Ignore the Rest

84. *Division of Investment Management: Report on Mutual Fund Fees and Expenses* (Washington, D.C.: U.S. Securities and Exchange Commission, 2000), <http://www.sec.gov/news/studies/feestudy.htm#item10> [accessed 20 April 2008].

85. Peter Lindmark, "Inactivity and Business Evolution," *GuruFocus*, 8 October 2007, <http://www.gurufocus.com/news.php?id=14681> [accessed 20 April 2008].

86. Dr. John Nofsinger, interviewed by author in Dallas, Texas, in 2004, <http://archives.kimsnider.com/archive.php?archive_id=127> [accessed 1 February 2008].

Chapter 17—Ignore Inflation at Your Peril

87. Kitty Bean Yancey, "Skiers Find Lots of Snow," *USA Today*, 14 December 2007, p. D1, <http://www.usatoday.com/travel/destinations/ski/2007-12-13-ski-trends_N.htm> [accessed 19 April 2008].

Chapter 18—Know your Greatest Risk

88. "The Importance of Personal Financial Protection" (American Council of Life Insurers, 2006), <http://www.acli.com/NR/rdonlyres/ DA6E28F0-3A2E-4039-963B-BCA9129DE03F/8649/ Personal_Financial_Protection.pdf> [accessed 1 February 2008].

89. Stacey L. Bradford, "Do You Need Disability Insurance?" *SmartMoney*, 19 April 2005, <http://www.smartmoney.com/insurance/disability/index. cfm?story=disability2005> [accessed 19 April 2008].

90. "Mandelbrot," <http://www.3villagecsd.k12.ny.us/wmhs/Departments/ Math/OBrien/mandelbrot.html> [accessed 27 December 2007].

Chapter 20—Take Care of Health Care

91. "Facts on the Cost of Healthcare" (American Council of Life Insurers, 2006), <http://www.acli.com/NR/rdonlyres/ DA6E28F0-3A2E-4039-963B-BCA9129DE03F/8649/ Personal_Financial_Protection.pdf> [accessed 1 February 2008].

92. Importance of Personal Financial Protection, ibid.

93. David E. Adler, "High Net Worth: The Long Goodbye," *Financial Planning*, 1 December 2007, <http://www.financial-planning. com/asset/article/528551/high-net-worth-long-goodbye.html> [accessed 28 December 2007].

94. "Press Release: 2007 National Long-Term Care Insurance Price Index Announced," *American Association for Long-Term Care Insurance*, 1 June 2007, <http://www.aaltci.org/subpages/media_room/story_pages/media070107. html> [accessed 28 December 2007].

95. Adler, ibid.

96. "2006 Long Term Care Insurance Sales and in Force" (LIMRA, 2007).

97. Charles Duhigg, "Aged, Frail and Denied Care by Their Insurers," *New York Times*, 26 March 2007, <http://www.nytimes.com/2007/03/26/ business/26care.html?_r=3&oref=login&pagewanted=print> [accessed 28 December 2007].

Chapter 21—Protect Your Identity

98. "A Chronology of Data Breaches," *Privacy Rights Clearinghouse*, 15 March 2008, <http://www.privacyrights.org/index.htm> [accessed 18 March 2008].

99. "Identity Theft Resource Center Facts and Statistics," *Identity Theft Resource Center*, 30 April 2007, <http://www.idtheftcenter.org/artman2/ publish/m_facts/Facts_and_Statistics.shtml> [accessed 18 March 2008].

100. Ibid.

101. Ibid.

102. Ibid.

103. Amy Buttell Crane, "Medical identity theft can kill you (page 3 of 3)," *Bankrate.com*, 5 January 2007, <http://www.bankrate.com/brm/news/ insurance/20070105_medical_identity_theft_a3.asp> [accessed 20 March 2008].

Chapter 22—Manage Your Credit Score

104. "National Average Credit Score," *Money-Zine*, <http://www.money-zine. com/Financial-Planning/Debt-Consolidation/National-Average-Credit-Score/> [accessed 20 March 2008].

105. Robert B. Avery, et al., "Credit report accuracy and access to credit," 2004, <http://econpapers.repec.org/article/fipfedgrb/y_3A2004_3Ai_3Asum_ 3Ap_3A297-322_3An_3Av.90no.3.htm> [accessed 20 March 2008].

SUMMARY

Four building blocks of financial success:

- Plan prudently
- Save prodigiously
- Invest wisely
- Manage risk

Three traits of financially successful individual:

- Determination
- Self-reliance
- Self-confidence

Your job as family CFO can be described by three activities:

- Planning
- Managing assets and liabilities
- Managing behavior

Three things that family CFOs must believe:

(1) You are accountable for your situation, today and tomorrow
(2) Your decisions will determine that situation
(3) Better decisions lead to better results

Planning activities include: goal setting, budgeting, quantifying goals, identifying and managing risks, and tax and estate planning

Planning activity I use in this book encompasses three things:

(1) Bringing the future into focus so we can affect it

(2) Reporting on the past so we know how we are doing

(3) Gathering outside knowledge so we can make good decisions

Managing assets and liabilities activity
Assets include:

- Stock portfolio
- Savings accounts
- Equity in your home
- 401(k)
- IRA
- Real estate
- Business

Liabilities are anything you owe to someone else. They include:

- Mortgage
- Car loans
- Leases
- Credit card debts
- Student loans
- Lines of credit

Net worth is the difference between your assets and your liabilities.

Managing behavior
(1) Living beyond your means
(2) Not saving for the future
(3) Taking unnecessary risk
(4) Relying on others to make important financial decisions for you
(5) Being uninformed

These behaviors can be by-products of such issues as self-esteem, self-control, approval seeking, and caretaking.

Move miles ahead on the path to financial freedom by having:
- A high-level objective
- Specific goals
- A plan for attaining those goals
- Detailed information from which you can monitor, track, budget, and plan

Financial success is a product of time, savings, and after-tax return.

Four factors to consider when deciding which investments to put your money to work in:
(1) Understand your money's higher purpose
(2) Consider where you fall on the risk-reward continuum
(3) Consider your temperament
(4) Consider your time horizon

In order to be a successful investor, you must learn how to
(1) Ignore your emotional response
(2) Train yourself to act opposite to what your emotions would tell you to do
(3) Adopt a rigid system that keeps you from responding emotionally

Three keys to rational investing:
(1) Control your environment
(2) Understand the different types of psychological biases
(3) Form a plan